the submariner's world

1

the submariner's world

1

Edited by Commander
P R Compton-Hall
MBE RN (Retired)

an annual underwater digest

kenneth mason

● The cover picture is of the Trident-carrying US Submarine Ohio (courtesy General Dynamics Corporation)

by the same author

Submarines Wayland 1982 (for children)

The underwater war 1939-45 Blandford 1982

Submarine boats Conway 1983

Naval warfare today and tomorrow (trans) Blackwell 1983

ISBN 0-85937 303-7

© **Commander R Compton-Hall 1983**

British Library Cataloguing in Publication Data

The Submariner's world. —1
    1. Submarine boats — Periodicals
    623.8'257'05   VM365

    ISBN 0-85937-303-7

Published by Kenneth Mason, The old harbourmaster's, Emsworth, Hampshire

Produced in Great Britain by Articulate Studios, Emsworth
Designed by Sadlergraphics

Printed in Great Britain by Redwood Burn Limited, Trowbridge, Wiltshire

Contents

Glossary

Submarines

AGSS	Auxiliary Submarine (eg for rescue or oceanological work)
APSS	Auxiliary Transport Submarine
ASSA	Auxiliary Cargo Submarine
ASSO	Auxiliary Oiler Submarine
DSRV	Deep Submergence Rescue Vehicle
DSSV	Deep Submergence Search Vehicle
DSV	Deep Submergence Vehicle
FBM	Fleet Ballistic Missile submarine (see also SSBN)
Guppy	Greater Underwater Propulsion Power (the name given to the fast USN diesel-electric submarines converted and streamlined from standard fleet boats after WW II)
HTV	Hull Test Vehicle (formerly NR-2) (nuclear propulsion)
IXSS	Miscellaneous Unclassified Submarine (alongside harbour training)
LPSS	Amphibious Transport Submarine
NR	Submersible Research Vehicle (nuclear propulsion)
SS	Submarine (usually implying diesel-electric propulsion)
SSA	Cargo Submarine
SSB	Ballistic Missile Submarine (nuclear propulsion) - colloq in RN 'Bomber')
SSG	Guided Missile Submarine (diesel-electric)
SSGN	Guided Missile Submarine (nuclear propulsion)

● The potential diversity of submarine tasks and operations is evident from the following list of abbreviations:

SSK	Patrol Submarine (diesel-electric) - 'hunter-killer'
SSM	Submarine Minelayer
SSN	Fleet Attack Submarine (nuclear propulsion) - 'hunter-killer' and colloq in RN 'Fighter' (as opposed to SSBN 'Bomber')
SSO	Submarine Oiler
SSP	Submarine Transport
SSR	Radar Picket Submarine
SSRN	Radar Picket Submarine (nuclear propulsion)
SST	Target and Training Submarine

Sensors and weapons

ABM	Anti-Ballistic Missile
ASROC	Anti-Submarine Rocket
ASUW	Anti-Surface Ship Warfare
ASW	Anti-Submarine Warfare
CBW	Chemical & Biological Warfare
CSDT	Control for Submarine Discharge Torpedoes
CW	Chemical Warfare
ECCM	Electronic Counter Counter-measures
ECM	Electronic Countermeasures
ELINT	Electronic Intelligence
ESM	Electronic Support Measures
FRAS	Free-Rocket Anti-Submarine
ICBM	Intercontinental Ballistic Missile

IFF	Identification, Friend or Foe
IR	Infra-Red
MAD	Magnetic Anomaly Detector
MIRV	Multiple, Independently Targetted Re-entry Vehicle
MRV	Multiple Re-entry Vehicle
NBC	Nuclear, Biological & Chemical
RNSH	Royal Navy Sub-harpoon
SINS	Ships Inertial Navigation System
SLAM	Submarine Air-Launched Missile System
SLBM	Submarine-Launched Ballistic Missile
SOSUS	Sound Surveillance System (ground array)
SSM	Surface to Surface Missile
USGW	Under Sea Guided Weapon

Escape

BIBS	Built-in Breathing System
DSEA	Davis Submerged Escape Apparatus
DSRV	Deep Submergence Rescue Vehicle
HIS	Hooded Immersion Suit
SEIS	Submarine Escape Immersion Suit
SET	Single Escape Tower

Foreword

Submarines today, especially when nuclear-propelled, are arguably the most powerful vessels at sea. Yet extraordinarily little is known about their true capabilities or about the submariners who man them. Underwater operations are necessarily secret: submarines depend upon remaining hidden and unseen for success, even in peace-time, and for survival in war. Hence, as a breed, submariners are not given, without persuasion, to discussing their way of life or even the reason for their spending weeks on end in an artificial world immersed in a hostile environment. Nor, come to that, are they worried about such things: they are entirely and demonstrably human even if they tend to develop a rather grey kind of humour which is peculiarly their own. There are many misconceptions about underwater warfare; and they are usually brought about by writers and critics who have little or no personal experience or knowledge of a highly specialised subject. It therefore seems high time to introduce submariners, internationally, as they really are — even if for no better reason than that nowadays both submarines and submariners are expensive and tax-payers everywhere will want to know what they are getting for their money. Is it money well spent? Are submarines, on all sides, as effective as they appear from the surface? The best way of answering questions like these is probably to look at underwater warfare and life below through the eyes of submariners themselves. That is the purpose of The Submariner's World which will be published annually with contributions duly wrung from the most silent of silent services around the world. I am most grateful to the contributors, many of them distinguished and busy men, who have written articles for this first volume and for the illustrations that have generously been provided from several sources. In particular, I thank the Trustees of the Royal Navy Submarine Museum at Gosport for permission to draw on the museum's vast collection of photographs.

Richard Compton-Hall
RN Submarine Museum, Gosport, Hampshire

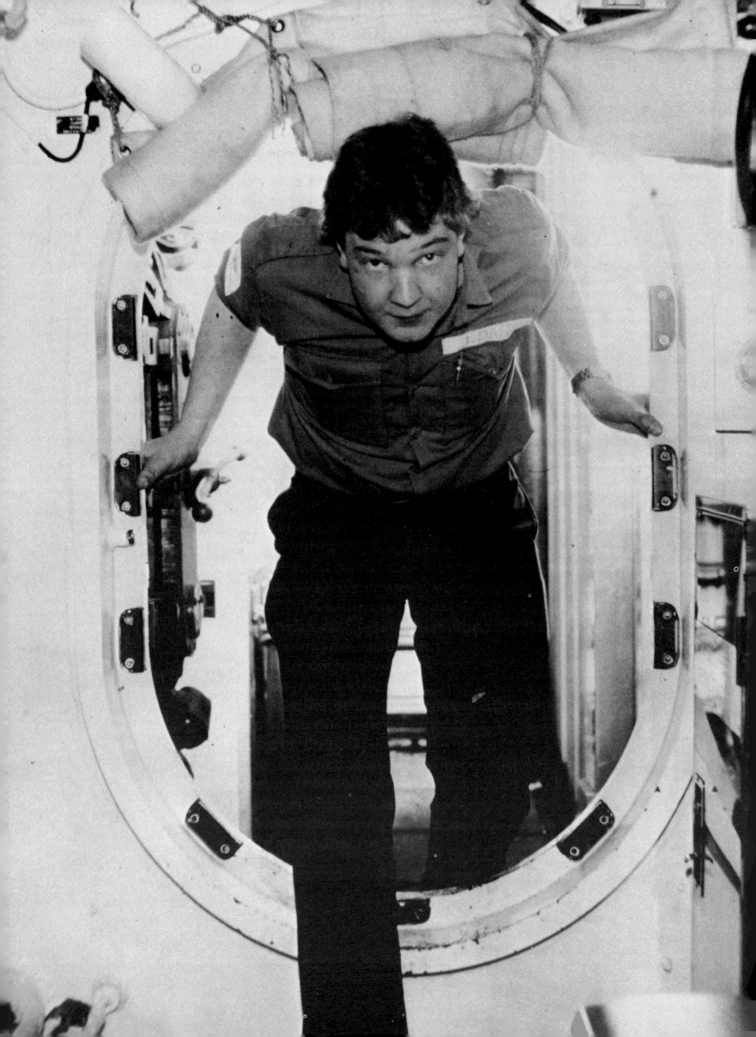

The submarine in 1984

by Admiral Sir Peter Herbert KCB, OBE, (Flag Officer Submarines and Comsubeastlant 1982-1983)

THE SUBMARINE OF 1984 seems to have little in common with its turn of the century predecessor. Yet the men who manned *Holland I* could identify with the modern submarine whose basic requirements remain unaltered — a weapon system with which to engage the enemy, a fire control system to direct those weapons, sensors with which to locate the target, a propulsion system to push the machine along, accommodation for the crew who operate those systems, enclosed by a watertight hull allowing it to justify its name and role.

Weaponry has developed from simple, straight-running torpedoes of comparatively short range to long range, guided underwater missiles such as *Tigerfish* and above water missiles like *Sub-harpoon*. Fire control systems have advanced from nothing more than the commanding officer's judgement and eye through simple mechanical units like 'fruit machines' to today's sophisticated computers. Sensors began with a periscope limited to the horizon but now encompass long-range active and passive sonars, Electronic Support Measures (ESM) equipment, periscopes with image intensification and the 'third party' — be it another maritime unit reporting a contact or various forms of intelligence. Nuclear propulsion has revolutionised the submariner's world, changing a slow vessel of restricted underwater endurance into a wide-ranging, fast, major warship of almost unlimited endurance, made of better materials whose fabrication has produced hulls capable of diving to greater depths. With all this has come vastly improved living quarters for the crew.

Although the main threat to peace comes from the Soviet bloc, until the 1950s their submarine force was unremarkable both as to capability and achievement. However the advent of nuclear power heralded a change in Soviet maritime strategy since when

their navy has expanded beyond recognition into a large, powerful, world-ranging force. Soviet submarines have been at the forefront of this expansion and their order of battle now includes some fine submarine classes, for example:

Alfa, a fast, deep diving SSN
Delta, a modern, large SSBN. When armed with the SS-N-18 missile, this submarine is capable of targetting Europe and the USA from its home waters in the vicinity of the Kola Inlet.
Typhoon, the largest submarine ever built, of the order of 30,000 tons. A brand new type of SSBN.
Oscar, a large (15,000 ton) SSGN armed with 24 SS-N-19 cruise missiles.

However, the Soviets do have problems. Their submarines are noisier than ours, their sonar technology less developed, their torpedoes less destructive and they have manpower problems. Whereas NATO's nuclear submarines are manned by career volunteers, the Soviets use a sprinkling of short-term conscripts, hence their training load is high. But they must not be under-estimated for those Soviet submarines which operate outside their home waters are professionally and competently handled, although but a small proportion of the total force.

To counter the Soviet threat, the UK has, first, the SSBN deterrent force, a squadron of four *Resolution* class submarines which has maintained at least one submarine continuously on patrol for some 15 years, no mean

In Thy hands! The captain of HMS Resolution, (then) Commander Colin Grant, gives the final authority, with his key, to launch missiles

achievement. Carried out with the minimum of publicity there has been little reward for the men involved, save recognition by higher command. That the aim of this force is to keep the peace is sometimes forgotten by those who protest its existence. Deterrence, by nuclear as well as conventional arms, is the best means of avoiding major conflict and the effectiveness of this SSBN force is fully recognised by the Soviet Union. Although ageing, the *Resolution* class has been updated regularly as have their missile systems. For instance, the recent introduction into service of the *Chevaline* system has marked a steep improvement in the effectiveness of the missile as a deterrent because the more effective a weapon is, the less willing is an enemy to have it used against him.

The future of the SSBN force lies with the *Trident* programme for the *Resolution* class and the Polaris missiles must be replaced some time in the mid 1990s. *Trident's* design is well advanced and incorporates much fascinating technological advance, an exciting prospect for future submariners.

Today's SSBN carries a comprehensive fit of sensors to provide long range early warning of the presence of possibly hostile forces, thus allowing the SSBN to avoid contact and remain unheard and unseen ready at all times to fire, should deterrence fail.

The SSN carries a similar fit of sensors but for a different purpose as she is the ocean hunter. The long range capability of today's sonar has exploited the latest techniques in electronics and acoustics although the propagation of sound below is only partially understood and research continues. Meanwhile, as Soviet submarines become quieter, (and the Soviet R-class was specifically built as an ASW weapon!), so sonar sensitivity must become capable of distinguishing submarine noise from the multitude of others in the sea. The capability of one submarine to detect, classify, close and attack another below periscope depth has been developed only in the last two decades.

It has come about with the introduction of reliable, highly capable homing torpedoes. The *Tigerfish* Mod O had its problems in the early stages but the *Tigerfish* Mod 1 is now capable of

Nuclear submarine bridges, because of essential streamlining, are generally cramped and uncomfortable: HMS Resolution, a fleet ballistic missile submarine, nuclear propelled, more commonly known as an SSBN, shown here is no exception

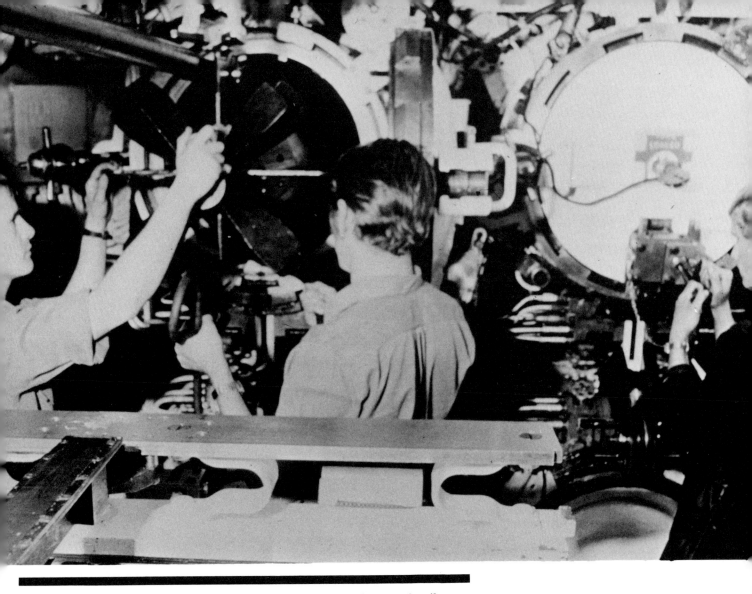

Loading a torpedo into one of the six bow tubes of a British SSBN. Torpedoes are primarily intended for self-defence: it is no part of SSBN policy deliberately to seek tactical engagements

attacking submerged submarines and surface targets. The ability to guide these weapons after firing gives them great tactical flexibility, should, for example, the target alter course. Feedback to the firing submarine includes details of contacts obtained and progress of the attack. Computerised fire control steers these torpedoes through evasive manoeuvres and decoys to destroy the target. *Spearfish*, the next generation of torpedo, offers even higher speed, greater range and better homing.

The SSN has gone full circle in its roles. At the beginning of the century submarines were capable only of attacking surface targets. In the 60s and 70s, the swing was towards attacking other submarines. Now, with the introduction into service of the *Sub-harpoon* the SSN has gained a much improved anti-surface capability. The development firings by two British SSNs on the Californian coast met with a success rate rarely equalled in weapon system development by any nation. The first RN submarine fully equipped to fire the missiles, *HMS Courageous*, subsequently took part in the Falklands campaign, although without firing in anger. As part of that campaign, the conversion of all SSNs to carry the missile was advanced so that this system is now at sea in several SSNs.

What of the SSK? The *Oberon* class is still the RN's work-horse. Considering the first design of the class dates from the early 1950s, it has proved a remarkably successful submarine. Rapidly drawing nearer is the 2400 class of new SSK, looking remarkably like a scaled-down SSN as it should, for in all but propulsion, it has an SSN's capabilities. It will carry the weapons, including *Sub-harpoon*, and the sensors of the SSN. With an improved battery endurance and a fast recharging capability, it will need to snort less frequently than today's SSK which will remain an essential element of the RN flotilla for it can carry out many of the tasks of the SSN, some better performed more economically. In wartime the SSK is ideally suited to patrolling static barriers covering various choke points, and in shallow water snorting infrequently. Its inherent quietness makes it difficult to detect. In peacetime the SSK can undertake many of the routine training functions, providing target facilities for other ASW forces at far less cost than the SSN. A sensible balance between SSNs and SSKs provides a cost-effective force capable of fulfilling all roles.

The primary commitment of RN submarines is to support NATO: thus exercises with submarines of other NATO nations are commonplace, in particular with the US and Netherlands navies, with whom our ties are very close. In addition, Norwegian, German, Danish, French and Portuguese submarines exercise around the waters of the British isles and we look forward to closer ties with the Spanish submarine force.

The early 1980s have seen some important advances in the NATO submarine force as a whole. The USN continues to expand the successful 688 (*Los Angeles*) class; the Netherlands will soon commission the first of the *Walrus* class of SSK; independently France has put her first French SSN, *Rubis*, into

service, with more to come. Spain has bought four *Agosta* class, and Italy is bringing the *Sauro* class into service. And in the eastern Mediterranean, Greece and Turkey now have a comprehensive force of 209s. Thus NATO as a whole has a modern well-balanced submarine force; those nations whose primary role lies in the deep eastern Atlantic (USA, UK, Netherlands and Portugal) operate a mix of SSBNs, SSNs and SSKs; nations whose role is to cover the shallower waters of Scandinavia or the more restricted waters of the Mediterranean have smaller SSKs, ideally suited to such areas.

The RN submarine flotilla has a primary role in the eastern Atlantic but must be capable of operating worldwide as recent events in the South Atlantic have demonstrated. Such commitments will continue although it will remain impossible to forecast where. Who would have predicted that the first live attack by an SSN would take place in a conflict between Britain and Argentina?

The importance of the Indian Ocean has grown over the last few years as the increasing Soviet presence there proves.

It is a task of the US, French and British navies to balance this presence for history has shown that the Soviet Union will exploit any weakness on our part to defend our right to free access and free trade across the oceans of the world.

I have written in enthusiastic terms about the capabilities of the RN submarine force in 1984 and its NATO counterparts and I make no apology for this. Although I believe our submarines to be excellent fighting vessels we dare not become complacent. The Soviet Union has fully recognised the worth of the submarine and has been, and still is, building them at a tremendous rate. Newer, quieter Soviet submarines must be countered by the best that NATO can muster. As Flag Officer Submarines, I have always taken quiet pride in the envy expressed by non-submariners in the quality and professionalism of our men. We insist on high standards, give young men a lot of responsiblity and see them respond to the challenge which is still the same for the young commanding officer taking his submarine to sea for the first time as it was for the young men of the 1900s.

HMS Olympus on the surface in a moderate sea. British O-Class patrol submarines have an excellent diesel-electric system that, although not giving them the speed and endurance comparable with nuclear power, is extremely quiet on main motors submerged and sufficiently quiet when snorting to guard against passive detection for a long while if the correct tactics are adopted. Although the 14 boats of this Class were commissioned between 1961 and 1967 and are coming to the end of their life-span, they are still powerful and effective units with excellent sonar and a weapon load of 20 torpedoes forward (Mk 8** and Tigerfish): the two stern tubes are no longer used — except as stowage for cans of beer!

HMS Swiftsure (SSN) (left) on her way to the Clyde from the submarine base at Faslane, Scotland. She was the first of six boats of this class commissioned between 1973 and 1981: they represent a considerable advance on the preceding Valiant class and are particularly quiet. Their diving depth is classified but is known to be great. The published speed is in excess of 30 knots while the core-life of the reactor has probably been increased. Although individual reloading of torpedoes can be accomplished in 15 seconds it is unlikely, with modern weapons such as the wire-guided Tigerfish, that rapid reloading would be necessary in practice: there are five torpedo tubes and 20 reloads are carried

Test Polaris missile-firing by British SSBN from the US Navy's East Coast range. Now equipped with multiple Chevaline nuclear warheads the 16 missiles carried onboard each submarine of the Resolution Class have a published range of about 4,630 Km. The Chevaline system includes advanced penetration aids (ABM-defeating). The SLBM has inertial guidance and is propelled by a two-stage solid propellant: its length is 9.55 m, launch weight 13,600 kg

The FBM way of life

● **This authoritative article, compiled from several sources, is provided by the US Submarine Force Library and Museum at the Naval Submarine Base, New London, Groton, Connecticut**

LIFE ABOARD a Fleet Ballistic Missile firing submarine, if not unique, is certainly different from that of all others. Where others measure time in days and weeks, the FBM crewman counts his in months. Months on patrol, months at home, months of training. His way of life is a mixture of about equal parts adventure, training, education, submerged isolation, family living, and the camaraderie of submariners the world over.

With nuclear power for propulsion, oxygen-generating equipment and air conditioning providing a controlled, pleasant and liveable atmosphere, FBM submarines are capable of almost endless periods of submerged patrols. Endurance of these true submarines, in fact, is limited only by the stamina of the crew. Taking full advantage of this revolutionary capability to keep the submarines on station as great a percentage of time as possible the Navy changed the traditional manning concept of one ship, one crew. Each FBM submarine is assigned two crews, called 'Blue' and 'Gold', each with its own skipper and full complement of officers and men. While one crew has the ship on patrol, the other is back in

USS George C Marshall (SSBN). Submarines mounting the strategic deterrent, of course, are not seen on the surface except when sailing for or returning from patrol: it is at these times that they are most vulnerable to attack and it may be necessary to increase protection for them at these critical periods However, there is no evidence to suggest that the opposition is capable of threatening them when actually in their secret patrol areas and an attempted war of attrition against them near their bases would scarcely be thought profitable in any conceivable circumstances at present

the home port, undergoing refresher training, taking leave, breaking in new members, and in general ready to go back to sea.

The Gold crew and an FBM submarine homeported in Charleston, South Carolina, is ready to take their submarine on patrol. Officers include the commanding officer, the executive officer, the navigator, the engineer and his three assistants, the weapons system officer and his assistant, the communicator, and the supply officer.

The crew of a *Lafayette*-class submarine consist of 124 men trained in a variety of skills. Average age of the crew is 24 and almost all are high school graduates. Everyone has received special training for submarine duty and all are volunteers. The ratings required aboard FBM's include electronics technicians, machinist's mates, electrician's mates and interior communications technicians to operate the nuclear propulsion plant. Fire control

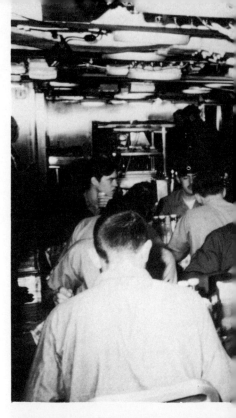

technicians, missile technicians and torpedomen maintain the ships' weapons systems. Sonarmen provide ears for the boat while quartermasters navigate and radiomen maintain listening contact with the outside world. Commissarymen, storekeepers, yeomen and hospital corpsmen provide the food service, administrative and medical support.

Each submarine squadron is supported by a submarine tender. When the submarine comes off patrol they pull alongside the tender for minor repairs, refitting, reprovisioning, etc. The Gold crew reports aboard the tender to live until their submarine comes in and the change of command has taken place. Then they move aboard her for the rest of the refit period. Alongside time runs about 30 days. The two crews get together immediately on return of the submarine and discuss the problems, plans, needed repairs and replacements, and so on. The crew change comes in a few days and the Blue crew departs to join their families. The Gold crew, together with that of the tender, then start on a round-the-clock schedule to ready the submarine for sailing. Despite long hours and hard work, the men get some opportunities to go ashore during this upkeep period.

A few days before patrol duty, the submarine is tested at sea to ensure that she and equipment are seaworthy. As scheduled, the submarine, complete with new crew, full provisions, and repairs made, slips away from the tender. All the crew know about the voyage is that they will be gone for about 60 days and will be submerged for the entire time. When they are to go, what route they will take, when they will return, only the skipper knows. But the whole crew is aware that the only reason for being on patrol is to be ready to launch their missiles if, and when, the President so orders. All the money, all the time spent in training, all the effort put into the system is for that sole purpose. By being on patrol beyond a potential enemy's ability to find and by being ready to launch missiles at any time, they know their ship is a mighty deterrent to an enemy attack.

As soon as they reach deep water they pull the plug to live, work, eat and play in an artificial undersea world for two months. Shortly after submerging,

the ship settles into the routine which will be followed for the entire cruise. Such routine is up to the skipper; in some cases watches are stood on a four hours on, eight hours off basis, but six hour watches are stood on most submarine patrols. The yeoman, corpsman, storekeeper, cooks, and some others may work normal ten to 12 hour days or split their work to cover periods required.

The submarine has been assigned a specific area to patrol and at all times is in range of assigned targets. Since the mission is to be ready to fire missiles on command, main emphasis of the daily routine is spent toward keeping the missiles in an 'up' status, ready to go. Missile firing drills are as much a part of life as eating and sleeping. Patrol experience has shown that FBM submarines average having 15 of their missiles ready for launch 99% of the time and all 16 of them over 95%. In addition to being ready to launch missiles, the submarine has to be ever alert to take evasive action if she detects strange ships, either submarine or surface, in her area. Each FBM submarine carries torpedoes as defensive weapons to protect herself.

Communications are the vital link with authority which can order missiles launched so radiomen keep round the

Control-room console, USS Ohio (SSBN 726) during a simulated missile firing during precommissioning training. The Ohio Class carry 24 Trident C-4 (UGM-96) SLBMs, half as many missiles again than earlier SSBNs, with a range of bout 7,000 km — approximately twice that of Poseidon. The greater range is acieved by a smaller and lighter guidance system which leaves more space for missile propulsion: a stellar sensor takes a star sight during the post-boost phase of flight and the post-boost vehicle corrects its flight path with data derived from this. Above is shown the crew's dining hall. It is not obvious that this is a submarine at all; the scene in a surface ship would be little different and the picture emphasises the huge size of the submarine which is 560 feet long, displacing 18,750 tons

clock vigil. Besides the need for getting the firing message should it ever be sent, the radiomen provide the only contact with the world outside. Daily news broadcasts by the Armed Forces Radio service are picked up and, what the crew considers more important — 'family-grams'. These are brief, personal messages from kin and friends of the crewmen which let them know how things are at home. An FBM submarine receives constant message traffic during a patrol but is not allowed to send any since it could give away her position.

Naturally, all is not work during patrol. Like all submarines, though bigger and roomier than Fast Attack submarines, bunks for all the crew are in the comparatively spacious crew's quarters. The captain and the executive officer have their own cabins. The officers double and triple up in well designed, but compact, staterooms. The ship is decorated throughout in light pastel colours to provide a pleasing atmosphere for the long haul. The crew's mess is large by submarine standards and serves the additional purpose of movie theatre, recreation hall, and study area.

Eating, of course, is of major concern, and every possible effort is made to provide outstanding food. This begins with the excellence of the cooks who are often given special training at top flight restaurants before joining a FBM crew. When the ship leaves home it carries enough food to more than cover the expected duration of patrol. Boneless and rationdense food are used to save storage space but submarines swear by the ability of the cooks to prepare a meal as fresh looking and tasting as you can get. Food consumption on a typical patrol will include something like 4,000 lbs of beef, 3,000 lbs of sugar, 1,200 lbs of coffee, 120 lbs of tea, 2,000 lbs of chicken, 1,400 lbs of pork loin, 1,000 lbs of ham, 800 lbs of butter, 3,400 lbs of flour, and 960 dozen eggs. Some of the more enticing items on the menu are Chicken Isabella, Baked Alaska, Shrimp Newburg, Beef Stroganoff and Lasagna. Standard favorites are roast beef and steak. Four meals a day are served including breakfast, lunch, dinner and a soupdown at midnight. The galley is open the rest of the time so everyone can help himself to sandwiches and snacks.

Exercise equipment is available on

17

most FBM submarines to help keep the weight down. Originally it was thought that boredom would plague the crew on long patrols like this, but it has not proven to be a problem. This is due to some extent to the long hours of hard work required on the part of every officer and man to keep the submarine ready at all times for its mission. Off hours are more than filled by the recreational facilities available, a well-stocked library, the need to study for advancement in rate, and, if desired, the opportunity to take college level courses for self improvement and college credit.

The submarine carries a good supply of movies and 'movie call' goes at least once a day, though usually twice to take care of day and night workers. Talent shows, bingo, and sing-along nights also help to enliven the cruise. All in all, the crew find that time passes quicker than expected and soon it is time to head back for home and turn the ship over to the Blue crew once again.

A few miles out from the tender the submarine surfaces and the men rejoin the work of ordinary mortals. Odd as it may seem, the first taste of 'fresh' air is not always appreciated since the controlled air of the submarine is cleaner and purer. A rash of colds may hit the crew right after return, too, for they have been free of such things since about a week after submerging on patrol.

Once alongside the tender, the Gold crew spends a few days handing over the ship to the Blue crew, and then they reverse the trip they took three months before. Arriving home, they may take leave if they want it. Like other Navy men, FBM crewmen get 30 days leave a year and usually split it between homeport periods. If they want they may take leave in Europe. After a week or two of getting used to home life, the crew starts on a regular five day a week program of refresher training.

Of particular importance is work in the elaborate FBM trainer which has been installed at the training facility at Charleston, for use by off crews. New members get a chance to work as a team with experienced personnel on equipment exactly the same as they will operate on patrol.

Family men, of course, spend as much time as they can with wives and children. One of the advantages of FBM life is that the men know what their schedule will be for the next year or so and can plan ahead with reasonable certainty. This is seldom the case with other men in any of the military services.

About one quarter of the crew will change during the off-patrol period with oldtimers going to shore duty or another submarine. Many will join precommissioning details of brand new FBM submarines which are still being built. Three months later the Gold crew will once again leave home and family, grass and sky, and return to the strange but exciting world beneath the sea.

The diving controls in the control-room of USS Ohio (SSBN) pictured during simulated diving operations in October 1981 before commissioning. Right, HMS Conqueror (SSN) at launch, Vickers, Barrow, August 28, 1969. Thirteen years later, on May 2, 1982, Conqueror (Cdr CL Wreford-Brown DSO) was to become the first nuclear submarine to sink a ship — the Argentinian cruiser General Belgrano

'The only answer to a nuclear submarine is another one'

Admiral Sir John Eccles, 1957

IN 1928 NO ONE could have foreseen that 54 years later a 250 bhp Brotherhood Burner Cycle radial engine was to have a greater impact on naval operations than any of the missiles which replaced Lord Fisher's big guns as the Fleet's main armament. However, that venerable but trouble-free, compact power-plant, neatly housed within a 21in diameter shell is still propelling the Mk VIII torpedo at speeds up to 45 knots with a degree of reliability which is the envy of its high-technology successors.

But in June 1945 when Commander A R Hezlet in *HMS Trenchant* scored five hits at a range of two miles in the last important attack of World War II to sink the Japanese heavy cruiser *Ashigara* no one expected our old stock torpedo to remain in service for long. True, it had scored 42% hits in the process of sinking more than 1,000 ships during the war, but surely something more effective would emerge as a spin-off from the missile age? So it was with some surprise that most old submariners learned that the salvo which, more than any other single incident, decided the Falklands naval campaign consisted of three Mk VIII **, spread for only one hit on the Argentinian cruiser *General Belgrano*, sank her with one in the fore-peak and one in the tiller-flat.

First reports suggested that wire-guided fish had been used from long range, but not so. Since the attacking submarine was the *SSN Conqueror*, 285 feet long with a 33-ft diameter pressure-hull and an enormous fin presenting an underwater target profile the size of a floating dock, everyone was impressed by the skill of her Commanding Officer (Commander C R L Wreford-Brown, DSO) in manouevring her undetected past the two escorting ex-American fleet destroyers in what seemed to be good

● by Captain John O Coote, RN (Retired) who writes on the part played by submarines in the Falklands campaign. The author joined submarines in 1942 and saw war service off Norway and in the Mediterranean and held four sea-going commands between 1948 and 1954 including HMS Totem where Lieutenant John Fieldhouse, now First Sea Lord, was his First Lieutenant. He left the Royal Navy at the age of 38 to go into newspaper publishing and ended as Deputy Chairman of Beaverbrook Newspapers. He still maintains his naval connections not least as a Trustee of the RN Submarine Memorial Museum at Gosport

sonar conditions, especially when it was leaked that the range on firing was a mere 1200 yards.

There are two clues to how this came about. Both centre around the enormous tactical advantage which the SSN's high speed, manouevrability and diving depth confer on her. This is so marked that our prospective submarine commanding officers are sent to sea in diesel boats to learn how to attack during their qualifying course (still called the 'Perisher' albeit with less justification than when the phrase was first coined). Otherwise, I am assured, it would be 'too easy'.

Equally, if an SSN is tasked to shadow and report an enemy, her simplest way would be from astern, either lying well back or shrouded by the underwater disturbance of the target's wake. To get into a point blank firing position from there would call only for a small helm order, a short burst of speed and the Mk VIII's angling gear to function within reasonable limits of accuracy.

The Naval Task Force Commander

(Rear Admiral Woodward flying in his flag in *HMS Hermes*) was, like his Commander-in-Chief (Admiral Sir John Fieldhouse), a submariner. So was the Assistant Chief of Naval Staff for Operations (Rear Admiral Tony Whetstone) and, of course, the Flag Officer Submarines himself (Vice Admiral Peter Herbert) in the underground HQ at Northwood, to which Fieldhouse had moved the Submarine Command's nerve-centre from Gosport a few years previously. Another happy coincidence which contributed significantly to the success of the whole campaign being conducted 8,000 miles away was that it so happened that it was a sailor's turn to be Chief of the Defence Staff (then Admiral of the Fleet Sir Terence Lewin).

By April 12, ten days after the Argentinians' invasion, Admiral Woodward already had three of his

HMS Conqueror returning triumphantly to her Faslane base flying the Jolly Roger to signify her exploits in the South Atlantic during the Anglo-Argentinian confrontation in 1982

allocated five SSNs on station to enforce the 200-miles Maritime Exclusion Zone around the Falklands. *HMS Spartan* (Commander J B Taylor) was the first to leave Gibraltar, making the dived passage to her operating area 6,500 miles away in less than ten days. She was closely followed by *HMS Conqueror, HMS Splendid* (Commander R C Lane-Nott), *HMS Courageous* (Commander R T N Best) and *HMS Valiant* (Commander T M le Marchant). Then, a long way behind, came the diesel-driven *HMS Onyx* (Lieutenant-Commander A P Johnson), but her submerged SOA was limited to eight knots, so she arrived in the area more than three weeks after the nuclear boats. This had to be accepted, but she must have been sorely missed in the early days of the campaign as a more suitable platform than any SSN for launching and recovering Special Boat Section (SBS) or SAS raiding parties. In the event she remained at sea for 116 days, which would have gone into the Guinness Book of Records but for the unusually tight security which still surrounds the movements of all our submarines.

For example, the C-in-C's Official Despatch on the South Atlantic Operations, published as a supplement to the *London Gazette* six months after the campaign ended, gives the precise date on which all naval units passed latitude 35° South and thus qualified for the campaign medal — except for the submarines.

Once the Total Exclusion Zone (TEZ) was established on April 30, coincident with the arrival of the main body of the Task Force, the SSNs were deployed to patrol its perimeter 200 miles out. By May 2 the Admiral had a clear picture of a pincer movement developing around the outer edge of the TEZ. Obviously the aim was to launch carrier-based air attacks from the *Vicento de Mayo* in the north, synchronised with ship-launched Exocet and 8in gun bombardment from the cruiser group in the south.

Conqueror had been tailing the *General Belgrano* for the best part of a day, while she patrolled an east-west line thinking herself immune from attack by remaining just outside the TEZ boundary. It is believed that she was waiting for an 'execute' signal from the carrier, who was hampered by thick fog. Although this enabled her to get past

HMS Spartan laying in wait for her, it also delayed the launch of her air strikes. But, while these major units remained on station, they posed a very serious threat to Admiral Woodward's carriers. The *Belgrano* tended to move into the relative safety of poor sonar conditions and shallow water on the Burdwood Bank. So permission was sought directly from Downing Street to vary the Rules of Engagement (ROE) and order *Conqueror* to take her out.

This she did with the utmost despatch, being sporadically depth-charged for her pains by the two Argentinian destroyers, who might more profitably have been employed in rescuing the cruiser's ship's company. Of the 321 thought to have died, many did so from hypothermia and should have been saved. *Conqueror* was under orders not to impede any rescue operations.

There was an immediate outcry that the sinking amounted to piracy. Left-wing politicians and TV pundits claimed that she was on a peaceful mission on a

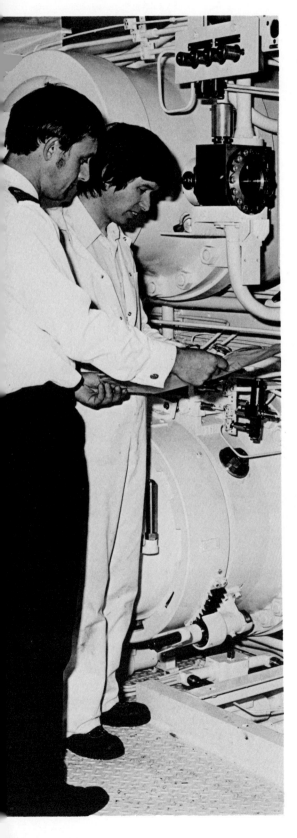

The price of a nuclear submarine is not confined to the hull. Realistic and intensive training is needed for every member of the crew and the cost is high for training facilities ashore like this Trafalgar-Class torpedo-tube arrangement in the Submarine School HMS Dolphin

westerly course heading for home. They saw the attack as having been triggered off by a hyped-up Mrs Thatcher, exasperated by futile shuttle diplomacy getting nowhere, except ever-extending CTF 317's logistics problems and sapping the stamina of his forces on station. Much has been written in the American press (North and South) about the high degree of intelligence data passed to our forces by the USA, even before they abandoned their 'even-handed' policy. In fact surveillance satellite coverage of the Falklands area was unreliable and of poor quality, certainly unable to offer our forces any guarantee against surprise attack.

But there is no doubt that the Argentine war plans for their naval forces were sufficiently well-known by the British High command from many different sources, some of which are not even hinted at in the C-in-C's Official Despatch. It is hard to believe that the Argentinian countermeasures against ELINT or SIGINT would be proof against modern methods of collection and processing.

What is admitted is that after the Argentinian Navy had turned for home on hearing of the loss of *Belgrano*, they were blockaded within their own 12-mile strip of territorial waters for the rest of the campaign by redeployment of our SSNs. The latter were also used thereafter to provide intelligence of enemy air movements to and from their mainland bases.

In another role, our submarines were responsible for putting ashore many of our special forces up to three weeks before the San Carlos landings. The white dagger on the Jolly Roger flown by *Conqueror* on her return to her home port was officially described as denoting a 'cloak-and-dagger' operation, meaning landing or recovering agents or special forces. An incident which has been expunged from the official records was the one-way mission of a Sea King helicopter which self-destructed on Chilean territory near Tierra del Fuego. The aircrew returned home by commercial air from Santiago, but their passengers disappeared into thin air somewhere in the vicinity of a nearby Argentinian Etendard airfield. They may well have been recovered by one of our submarines on completion of their mission.

Throughout the campaign our SSNs kept a special look-out for the two Salta class submarines. They were German-built, of recent origin, diesel-electric, small, very quiet on their motors and armed reportedly with sophisticated weapons and sensing equipment. Extravagant claims for the ease with which they penetrated our ASW screens have appeared in international defence publications, both as articles and as paid advertisements. Torpedo tracks were reported, and no doubt the whale's mating grounds were alive with acoustic red herrings (if the expression may be forgiven). But I have it on good authority that, once the ex-Guppy *Santa Fé* had been sunk off South Georgia, our ASW forces had not a single confirmed submarine contact throughout the campaign.

It may also be assumed that at least one of our SSNs acted as sonar picket or close screen for the aircraft-carrier group, using techniques first developed during Operation Rum Tub in the North West Approaches in October, 1957. Then *USS Nautilus*, a rather noisy, 22-knot, twin-screw boat, successfully defended the carrier *HMS Bulwark* against all attacks by our conventional submarines.

Argentinian commentators have already emphasised the hopelessness of their SSK's task when pitted against nuclear submarines and put this factor high on the list of why their navy failed. A quarter of a century ago our C-in-C Home Fleet (the unforgettable Admiral Sir John Eccles) wrote to the First Sea Lord, 'So long as *Nautilus* behaved in a conventional manner, our equipment came up to expectations, but just as soon as she developed her full capabilities she had the freedom of the seas . . . The only real answer to a nuclear submarine is another one . . . Time is not on our side.'

HMS Dreadnought was laid down two years later.

What submariners are paid

	Daily Rate	Submarine pay (extra)
Fleet Chief Petty Officer Artificer	£33.49	
Fleet Chief Petty Officer (other)	£30.85	£4.73
Charge Chief		£4.73
Chief Artificer after three years	£32.18	
Chief Artificer	£30.96	£4.73
Chief Petty Officer (other)	£29.80	£4.73
Petty Officer Artificer	£27.31	£4.73
Petty Officer (other)		£4.73
Leading Artificer	£26.24	
Leading Rate	£24.42	£3.93
Able Seaman		£3.93
Sub Lieutenant (GL)	£20.71	
Lieutenant (GL)	£21.96	£3.93
Lieutenant Commander (GL)		£3.93
Commander	£16.91	
	£22.78	£3.57
	£30.87	£4.73
	£39.69	£5.11
	£51.37	£5.11
		£5.11

Rates are lower rates for ratings and mid-seniority rates for officers
The daily rate of Command money is £1.00

Trident: the Polaris successor

● by John Chambers, the RN Submarine Command PRO between 1973 and 1978, who is now the Clyde Naval Information Officer based at Faslane where he spends much of his time responding to public interest in the intention to develop the Clyde Submarine Base for Trident

THE NEED FOR a UK strategic-deterrent system to take-over from *Polaris* in the 1990s first reared its head in 1962, when Britain bought into the submarine-launched ballistic missile programme with the signing of the Nassau Agreement.

Most people would say that a 30-year stretch on the life of (what was then) almost-entirely new British conceptual, design, engineering and material development is really good value for money.

Traditional schools of thought might have prophesied a 20-year life, even though *Polaris* captains do not drive their boats so exuberantly as their hunter-attack opposite numbers and the 'bombers' weren't going to get wore-out so quick.

Nevertheless a point must come when no matter how much tender loving care and money is invested in refits, modifications and add-ons, 30-year-old submarines and rockets will eventually look threadbare as the Nation's Ultimate Line of Defence.

Without rehearsing the arguments on deterrence theory, at least one central, practical fact is inescapable: it is not enough that a Government should deploy kit which has a pretty devastating ring to the Green Peace People and the CND; it is 'the opposition' that has to be impressed.

It would ill-behove us to under-estimate the professional and analytical talent available to the Kremlin. Once upon a time they may arguably have been somewhat astern of the west in their own submarine development and their mastery of the state of the underwater arts. But those days are over and the Soviet 30,000 ton, 20-tube *Typhoon*-class *SSBN* — of which the first was launched in 1980 — fairly demonstrates the fact.

In the final analyses, a British contribution to strategic deterrence has meaningful relevance only if the Praesidium is being advised by their own experts that it must be taken seriously: that the edges of the question marks posed against the temptation to adventure are as sharply and starkly defined as they ever were.

In simplistic terms, for newcomers, if a deterrent is to be convincing, certain things have to be demonstrated by the operator like competence, confidence and determination. On top of that most of the normal rules of mechanics, physical properties and existing design standing up against new developments also bear:

Is the composite system likely to be so reliable as to be capable of returning to sea, on schedule, time after time?

Is it reliable as to be capable of sustaining its patrol pattern at sea without risk of disruption by defects incurable at sea?

Is it going to continue to be technically so hard to locate for the foreseeable future that, still, it must be categorised as 'invulnerable'?

If ever it sought to launch its missiles, does the quality of the system make it likely that all would work as required and the missiles perform to specification?

Do the re-entry clusters have characteristics which make it impossible to guarantee to interdict the missiles en route to their designated targets once they are launched?

If the answers to these questions (and more of like kind) are judged by the opposition's analysts to be 'yes', only then may it be said that a submarine-borne deterrent is worth its rations.

Running the risk of undue repetition, because it is certain that this central issue often does not occur even to the most sensible people unless it is emphasised: A deterrent can only be credible if the likelihood of it working is rated, **in the calculation of those against whom it is ranged,** to be some substantial number of levels higher than the hope or off-chance that it might not work.

The point when the Yes-es begin to become slightly blurred around the edges may be said to be the point that Britain approaches in the 1990s.

The *Resolution*-class boats are now embarked on a cycle of third refits. We can certainly conjecture that these will be pretty costly enterprises, involving rather more than just a re-buffing of the brightwork. But there has to be a limit somewhere . . . and even if the hull could be pushed (on an expense-no-object basis) for yet more years, the crunch comes with the weapon itself. It is now 23 years since *Polaris* began to enter USN service: by 1995 it will be 35 years old. Few family cars are on the

Submarine model-making is becoming increasingly popular: the Association of Model Submariners was formed in 1982 to cater for those interested in making working models. This is a 1:48 scale model of HMS Tabard before conversion. The Secretary of the Association is Roger Serpell, 25 Onslow Road, Richmond, Surrey

Model by Lieutenant Colonel P Bowers of the Rev George William Garrett's steam-driven submersible Resurgam built in 1879 at Liverpool. Lost under tow off the North Wales coast in 1890 (with nobody on board) the Resurgam is now being searched for: when found it is intended to salvage the little boat and bring her to the RN Submarine Museum at Gosport (Lieutenant Colonel F V P Bowers)

road at that age, even as old bangers.

The RN *Polaris* certainly remains effective for the time being: the Chevaline front-end and the re-motoring programme have done what was necessary to ensure its performance for the requisite decade-and-a-bit that it must remain on duty. 'Instant pundits', looking for room to manoeuvre within the *Polaris*-successor controversy that hallmarks the summer of 1983 (as these words are being written), sometimes try for a balancing act on deterrence-without-*Trident* along the lines that it ought not to be impossible to extend further *Polaris* into the 'twenty-hundreds' with some sort of refurbishment programme; but fabricating major replacement components is not something you do at the friendly neighbourhood garage in the lunchbreak.

By the late 1990s, Polaris will be a production line that was laid-off two decades previously. It will not simply be a matter of cranking-up sheds still laid out neatly with dusty multi-million dollar machinery left standing dormant for 20 years plus on some quiet back-lot. Imagine trying to resuscitate the British aerospace industry of the late 1950s.

Indeed, the recent programme to re-motor *Polaris* had to surmount the fact that a considerable number of original contributing suppliers — and some hundreds had long gone out of the missile business — were untraceable.

Nor are plant and surviving industrial infrastructure enough on their own. Experience and expertise in handling 'old time' materials, would be a key element in the cost/effectiveness equations. Septuagenarians had to be brought out of retirement even to make the recent re-motoring programme possible; a 1990s roll-call might have to be conducted in the graveyard. No doubt the engineering world then will be capable of working from the same blueprints, and meeting the same quality-control standards as their forerunners of 30 years previously. But in the electronic-system field alone, a bulk-run component bought in at $18.50 in the 1960s, in 1983 would cost a short-run item price of $10,000 per copy.

It must be accepted that Britain's *Polaris* force will have come to the end of its career before the present century takes its bow. That is not an argument, of course, that there *has* to be a *Polaris* successor. The question of follow-on is a political decision. Nor does it automatically have to be a second-generation submarine-launched ballistic missile choice.

But it is certain that, since these things take ten-15 years to gestate from concept to entering operational service, the necessary decisions must be taken now. We are responsible for our people's security in the year 2000 and onwards. The argument ostensibly rages around whether there should be a successor deterrent at all (or, indeed, whether what we have should be

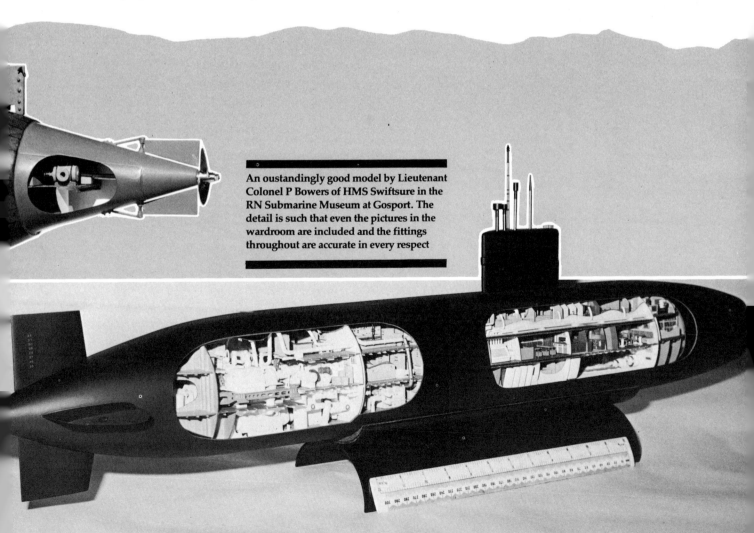

An oustandingly good model by Lieutenant Colonel P Bowers of HMS Swiftsure in the RN Submarine Museum at Gosport. The detail is such that even the pictures in the wardroom are included and the fittings throughout are accurate in every respect

summarily phased-out forthwith). With Cruise holding centre-stage at the time of writing, the *Trident* debate does little more than reverberate pianissimo in the background.

An assumption must be risked that those who acquire a submarine year-book will have an above-average wish to be authoritatively informed, and that anyone choosing to read this particular article has at least some minimal determination to see if there is anything new on offer on the *Polaris*-successor topic.

In July, 1980 the UK Government announced the decision to buy the *Trident* missile system to replace *Polaris*. On March 3, 1981, the House of Commons, by 316 votes to 248 approved that decision and endorsed the choice.

The record of the March, 1981 debate is not often referred to by the anti-*Trident* lobby. In some cases this is from ignorance. In others there may even be wilfulness in allowing the impression to generate that *Trident* has been simply rubber-stamped on Ministerial say-so— 'yet another' behind-closed-doors rape of democratic principles. It happens not to be true. But that does not necessarily make it a popular fact of life.

Nor is the Westminster endorsement the product only of a single debate: On January 24, 1980 the Secretary of State for Defence (Mr Francis Pym) introduced what might be called the 'foundation' debate in the *Trident* portfolio [*Nuclear Weapons, Hansard Volume 977, No 1021*].

On March 3 1981, the *Trident* Debate, the Secretary of State for Defence (Mr John Nott) moved that the House should endorse 'the Government's decision to maintain a strategic nuclear deterrent and the choice of *Trident* missile system as the successor to the *Polaris* force' [*Nuclear Deterrent — Hansard Volume 1000, No 291*].

From there it is possible to move on to what may be termed the technical pedigree of the *Trident* decision itself. There is a substantial and substantive bibliography accessible to whosoever chooses to seek it out, and quite separate from the 'Nuclear Titles' — especially those with an anti-nuclear leaning — recently described as the publishing growth-industry of 1983.

The need to make *Polaris*-successor decisions has crystalised at the most confusing of times. It is as if whimsical gods had predisposed that all the controversies of MX, Cruise, Pershing, SS20, *Trident, et al* should break around an alarmed mankind's ears simultaneously, to be confounded further by the heartsearching resulting from the lessons of the South Atlantic. And then Comrade Brezhnev has to die in the middle of it all, clearing the way for a successor seemingly more talented and willing to engage in exercises of global sleight-of-hand.

Acknowledging that these times are not the most propitious for clear-headedness, what explanation other than recklessness or a wish to misinform, or sheer incompetence, can there be in declamations such as, '*Government plans to build at least five Trident submarines*'; the new *Trident II* missile '*will carry 24 warheads*'; or an insistence that '*with Trident II Britain will have 896 warheads at sea at any one time, compared with the 48 or, at most, 96 with Polaris*' (or, presumably, 1,920 if the 24 warheads in 16 tubes in five boats becomes the disinformation vogue!).

Four British *Trident* submarines are planned: *Trident II* has a capability of *up*

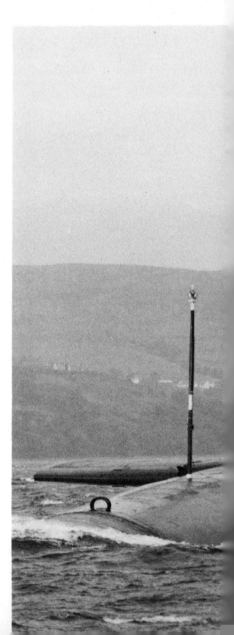

HMS Resolution pays-off from Faslane on August 20, 1982, on passage to Rosyth to enter her third refit since commissioning in October 1967. As she set course down the Gareloch, her port-side missile hatches were opened in sequence to spell out the submariner's farewell message to shore-side watchers
'Sea power for peace'

to 14 re-entry vehicles (Fourth Report Session 1980-81 House of Commons Defence Committee Page xii, para 24); while the Government gives an under-taking *that the move to Trident D5 will not involve any significant change in the planned total number of warheads associated with our strategic deterrent force in comparison with the original intentions for a force based on the C4 missile system.* (Defence Open Government Document 82/1 March, 1982, para 30). Indeed maximum C4 capability is eight re-entry vehicles. Once all four have been built and with one boat in refit at any one time, *up to 384*

warheads might be deployed in the Trident operational cycle (ie not all would be at sea on operational patrol concurrently) only if the full C4-equivalent capability was being taken up with warheads. The nominal Polaris A3 in cycle capability is of the order of 144 warheads, with no published nominal capability given for Chevaline.

What responsible information is available when every Centre for Strategic Research or Institute of Defence Studies seems to be having a go, but not necessarily agreeing even with each other? There is one source reasonably and logically in possession of

all the background equations to the *Trident* decisions; the UK Ministry of Defence, where professional staffs, made up of all sorts of conditions of ordinary citizens engaged in an a-political, technical job, have spent years working progressively on the *Polaris*-successor studies.

It needed their research to define the options for political decision. With the decisions made, Mr Pym and Mr Nott, as successive Secretaries of State, were in a position to authorise a number of helpful public papers for issue. Two are of notable significance:

Defence Open Government Document 80/23 (July, 1980), *Britain's Strategic Nuclear Force: The Choice of a System To Succeed Polaris;* and Defence Open Government Document 82/1 (March, 1982) *The United Kingdom Trident Programme.*

Both are available from Ministry of Defence/DPRS, Main Building, Whitehall, London SW1A 2AH. Written for non-specialists their length is modest. Far from being propaganda blurbs, they are official papers formally tabled for the information of Parliament by the Secretary of State, with all the traditional responsibility to Parliamentary accountability that that embodies.

Yet even if the Ministry were the only repository of *all* the information to be taken into account, the Ministry must not be considered beyond challenge.

Parliament has the power to enquire and it has done so. More than 350 pages of argument and evidence for and against *Trident* are recorded in two Reports compiled by the House of Commons Defence Committee in the course of an investigation into *Strategic Nuclear Weapons policy.*

In its *Fourth Report Session 1980-81* (HMSO 36/674 (1970-80, ISBN 0 10 203681 £10.60)) and in its *First Special Report Session 1981-82* (HMSO HC266/ HC266-I, ISBN 0 10 226682 (£4.25)) the Committee correlates the verbatim evidence for which it had called: it has substantial constitutional inquisitorial powers. The Fourth Report includes a summary of conclusions and recommendations.

Nearly a year

The Committee took 11 months over the *Fourth Report* investigations — from June 1980 to May 1981, when the House of Commons ordered it to be printed.

In the course of its studies, the Committee records that it took evidence on 'The Choice'. The Report's Contents itemises: *Trident . . . Cruise missiles . . . Updated Polaris . . . Anglo-French Co-operation . . . The Government's Choice . . . Boats on Station and the Fifth boat . . . The New Class of Submarine and the Force Options . . . Propulsion Plant . . . Missiles and Number of Tubes . . . The Trident I (C4) Option . . . The Trident II (D5) Option . . .* And this leads on to headings of *Cost . . . Management . . . Timescale . . . etc,* and thus to the Committee's *Summary of Conclusions and Recommendations.*

The introductory section consists of some 16 pages of reading which tends to surprise those encountering it for the first time.

The subsequent *First Special Report* covers further submissions to the Committee following the Government's announcement on March 11, 1982 that the decision had been taken to procure *Trident II (D5).* It details a further meeting between the Committee and the Secretary of State for Defence (Mr Nott) and a number of his advisors.

In paragraphs 3 and 4 of the *Fourth Report* narrative, the Committee summarise the range of their activity: *'We have taken evidence on no less than 14 occasions. In addition to Ministry of Defence witnesses and the Secretary of State for Defence, we heard evidence from Mr David Greenwood, the Director of the Centre for Defence Studies at Aberdeen University, from Colonel Jonathan Alford and Dr Desmond Ball of the International Institute for Strategic Studies (IISS), British Shipbuilders, Rolls Royce and Associates, British Aerospace Dynamics Division and the Society of British Aerospace Companies. We made visits to the Clyde Submarine Base at Faslane where the Polaris boats are based; to Rosyth to see the current arrangements for refitting nuclear ballistic missile submarines (SSBNs); to Cammell Lairds, Birkenhead and Vickers, Barrow shipyards where the Polaris Submarines were constructed; and to the Atomic Weapons Research Establishment at Aldermaston where the nuclear warheads for Trident will be developed. We also invited written evidence from a number of interested individuals. A full list of witnesses whose written and oral evidence has been published by the Committee is given on pp ixvii to lxx.*

In March 1981 the Committee went to the United States in order to make visits to the Headquarters of Strategic Air Command at Omaha, Nebraska, where the Joint Strategic Target Planning Staff is located and the United States manned strategic bomber and land based ballistic missile force is controlled; to Washington for discussions on strategic nuclear weapons policy and arms control with Congressional Committees, the Department of State and the Department of Defence and for briefings on the Trident system from the United States Navy; and to the King's Bay, Georgia base whence Trident missile carrying submarines are deployed. We delayed the completion of our Report until we had had the opportunity to make this visit and we believe that the information gained there has fully justified the delay.'

The catalogue of witnesses, memoranda and appendices fills some two and a half printed pages and is too long to reproduce. Overall, if someone in the writer's position may risk a careful comment on Parliamentary affairs, it may be said that the Committee would appear to have gone about its business most thoroughly indeed.

To complete the picture as of this date one should add:

The texts of the letters exchanged between the UK and US Governments on the procurement of *Trident D5 (The British Nuclear Force, March 1981;* HMSO Cmnd 8517 (£1.15));

The statement made by the Secretary of State for Defence (Mr Nott) in announcing the *Trident D5* decision (Hansard Volume 19 No 751, columns 975-986); and

The statement made by the Secretary of State for Defence (Mr Nott) in announcing the decision that the UK *Trident* 'Short missile' (the motor stages) would be prepared and refurbished at King's Bay, Georgia, under arrangements made with the US Government.

Read and digest

By way of an interim conclusion, on a subject still with much of its course to run, the sum total of Parliamentary and Parliament-orientated papers which have been cited certainly are available as basic reading for anyone setting out to form serious and sober opinions on the *Trident* choices which have been made.

For most people, however, it is easier to fall back on the pre-digested 'instant education' preferred by the media — which is not necessarily intended as direct criticism, since even the most gifted and impartial 1,500 words or 57 minutes of video simply cannot encompass the full scope of the many technicalities involved and of the balances which have to be struck somewhere in making decisions of such magnitude with an eye on the needs of a half-century ahead.

In essence, as of the date of closing this article (June 1983) there is nothing particularly 'new' to be said about the UK *Trident* programme. Perhaps just quite a lot to be re-discovered — information for professionals to think about.

An opinion by the Civil Service

THIS DEPARTMENT considers that, in general, it is safe to assume under most circumstances (provided no factor that might be prejudicial is present) that the chances are, in reasonable conditions, that a fair measure of success may be obtained. A not unsatisfactory performance may in fact be achieved for an indefinite period, depending on a number of unpredictable factors. Should, however, this not actually appear to be the case, (which can be stated to be not entirely improbable though not at the same time altogether likely) it would possibly indicate the conditions to be such that not too much reliance should be placed on the results.

● Eventually, submarine officers, in any navy, find themselves transported to the Ministry of Defence, or its equivalent, where they are forced to fight the implacable Civil Service with pens and dockets and seek opinions from the mandarins. This is reputed to be one such opinion in answer to a straightforward question

The fact that they might on the other hand be excellent should not be overlooked.

It is therefore felt that without extensive trials it is difficult to advance a definite opinion. Such trials, if conclusive, might afford information on which it would be possible to base an estimate — on the other hand they might prove unproductive.

Until confirmation has or has not been established by such trials it is requested that these remarks should be treated with reserve, and it is realised that they are not the last word on a subject that must, after all, be viewed from many angles and appropriate action be taken by the authorities on the spot to meet the particular circumstances of the case.

Submarine nuclear power plants

THE SUCCESSFUL development of nuclear power plants for naval use has transformed the submarine's war-time role. Despite the invention of the schnorkel, the conventional submarine is still a vessel which must return frequently to within, perhaps, 20 ft of the surface of the ocean, is limited by battery power to a few hours of relatively slow speed when diving deep, and limited to about ten weeks endurance at sea by the need to carry fuel.

Because the fission energy obtainable from uranium or plutonium is about a million times more per pound of fuel than that obtainable from the combustion of fuel oil, and does not

● by Cliff Horton, Managing Director of Rolls-Royce and Associates Limited who are responsible for the design, manufacture and service support of nuclear submarine power plants for the RN. Originally a physics graduate in research at the UK Atomic Energy Establishment, Harwell, he moved to Rolls-Royce to take part in the submarine development programme in 1957, where he was Chief Physicist and later Technical Manager during the development of the first nuclear submarines for the RN. After appointments as Computing Manager and Director of Production Control with the aero-engine business of Rolls-Royce, he returned to Rolls-Royce and Associates Limited in his present post in 1980.

require the presence of oxygen to be released, the nuclear submarine can remain submerged indefinitely — for all practical purposes — and has an endurance at sea measured in hundreds of weeks. Moreover, the design of the hull can be optimised for underwater 'flying' (Fig 1), rather than for surface sea-keeping, and there is sufficient power available from the nuclear reactor to drive advanced sonars, computers, navigation equipment and air conditioners, as well as to propel the submarine at underwater speeds to match most surface vessels.

The submarine nuclear power plant has been developed so far to power a wide range of vessels in the American, British, French, Russian and Chinese navies, from the relatively small *USS Skate* (2,500 tons) to the gigantic Russian *Typhoon* class at a reported 30,000 tons (Fig 2). *Jane's Fighting Ships* confidently assigns speeds of 30 knots and diving depths of 300 metres to the modern nuclear-powered attack submarine, speeds that can be sustained indefinitely.

What are the probable lines of development of the submarine nuclear power plant for the future?

Present state of art

The present submarine nuclear power plants generate heat from nuclear fission in a core containing uranium, and use a heat transfer medium to transfer it in a closed primary circuit to a heat exchanger. The heat exchanger forms the heat source for a steam generator in a closed secondary circuit — in which water is boiled to form steam to drive steam generators and turbo-generators — the exhaust of which passes through sea-water condensers and is pumped back to the inlet of the steam generator (Fig 3).

During operation of the reactor, some components — the primary heat transfer medium and corrosion products within it — become radio-active from exposure to the neutron flux within the reactor; it is the purpose of the separate primary circuit to contain these active elements within a high-integrity boundary in a separate reactor compartment.

Both water under pressure (to suppress surface boiling) and liquid metals (sodium or sodium/potassium mixtures) have been used as the primary circuit heat transfer medium. The latter was demonstrated in the power plant of the *USS Seawolf*, but was later abandoned due to the difficulty of coping with leaks at the sodium/water interface in the steam generator. The technology of the pressurised water reactor (PWR), however, has now been extensively developed and forms the basis for

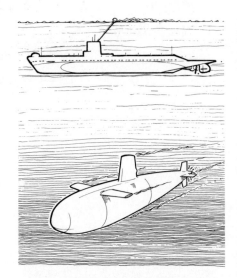

Figure 1. Speed and noise reduction demand the tear-drop or porpoise shape for nuclear hulls which were first tested in the high-speed (25 kts) conventional submarine USS Albacore (AGSS 569) completed in 1953. It is similar to the shape conceived as ideal by J P Holland, the Irish-American father of modern submarines, towards the end of the last century

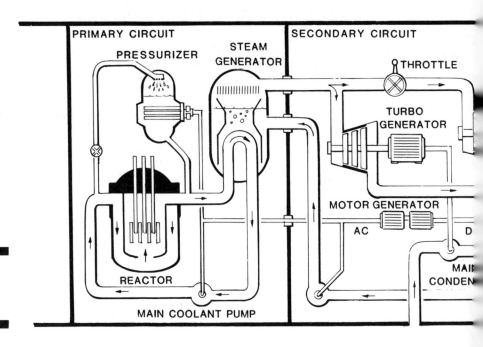

Figure 3. Schematically, a nuclear power plant is not difficult to understand: in engineering and mathematical terms it is elegantly simple

today's nuclear submarine fleets. In the course of this development, the designers have learned how to make leaktight welds in the thousands of primary circuit components, pumps have been developed which run for many thousands of hours without attention, and reactor technology allows the construction of reactors which will run for years between refuels and which respond readily to power demands.

Future developments

To some extent, the development of the submarine nuclear power plant of the future will depend on the requirements and resources of the navy concerned rather than the state of reactor technology. In addition to the individual ship requirements of power (speed), noise and diving depth, the cost of each ship will determine the fleet requirement and deployment (Fig 4). As we have already seen, the technology of today can be applied to a wide range of hull sizes; the choice between relatively few high-speed, deep-diving submarines or a larger fleet of smaller, slower and cheaper vessels is as much a strategic decision as a technical one.

Bearing these points in mind, we can still review the direction in which technology may be expected to develop in respect of endurance, speed, noise and diving depth within the next decade or so.

Endurance

The transfer of heat from the core to the primary heat transfer medium is driven by the temperature difference between the core and the medium concerned, and the area of fuel exposed to the heat transfer medium. The temperature of the fuel must be restricted within certain limits to avoid damage, so that there is a practical lower limit to core size of a few hundred litres for submarine nuclear power plant application.

One year of full speed operation of a typical submarine will consume a litre or so of uranium fuel, so that it is clear that there is no problem in finding storage space for this fuel in the reactor core. However, as the fuel is consumed, the changing distribution of power in the core leads to 'hot spots' which must be avoided to prevent fuel damage. The design of the reactor to avoid this problem presents an intensely difficult challenge, but the techniques are now sufficiently well understood that there is no sound theoretical reason why a naval nuclear power plant should not be built with any desired endurance. Practically, however, the time taken to refuel the submarine is relatively short compared with the time required for a major refit, and the endurance of today's submarines is already such that refuelling can be carried out during refitting. It is unlikely, then, that the extension of endurance will be a major development for the future.

Speed

The underwater speed of a submarine depends on the reactor power available, the hull shape, efficiency of conversion of reactor heat to propulsive power at the propellor, and the efficiency of the propellor design. All the engineering problems concerned are being studied energetically, and many improvements have been made since the early designs: notably the *Albacore* shape of the *USS Skipjack* class of attack submarines.

There are, however, a number of fundamental problems which the designers must face.

First, the drag exerted by the water on the hull increases enormously with increasing speed: to double speed from 20 knots to 40 knots requires eight times as much power at the propellor. Secondly, since the power requirement has increased much more than the flow of sea-water past the steam condensers, it becomes more difficult to reject waste heat to the ocean. Lastly, both propellor and hull noise increase dramatically, as does the temperature of the sea in the wake of the submarine (Fig 5). The last two phenomena, of course, effectively increase the range over which the submarine can be detected, which tends to offset the benefits gained by increased speed.

A doubling of reactor power is probably achievable from today's PWR technology by careful attention to the detailed design of the components, and this would lead to improvements in speed of around 25%. In this way, we could expect to see the present speed range of the nuclear submarine extended from 20 - 30 knots to, perhaps,

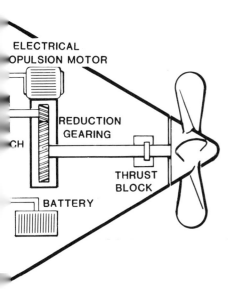

ELECTRICAL
PROPULSION MOTOR

REDUCTION
GEARING

CH

THRUST
BLOCK

BATTERY

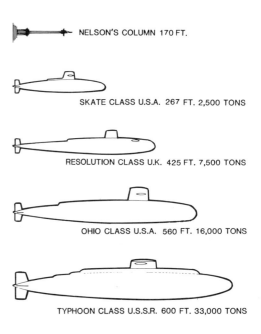

NELSON'S COLUMN 170 FT.

SKATE CLASS U.S.A. 267 FT. 2,500 TONS

RESOLUTION CLASS U.K. 425 FT. 7,500 TONS

OHIO CLASS U.S.A. 560 FT. 16,000 TONS

TYPHOON CLASS U.S.S.R. 600 FT. 33,000 TONS

25 - 35 knots in the near future, but it is unlikely that significant further improvements will be made without major investments in new technology. Possible ways ahead are the development of the high-temperature gas primary circuit directly coupled to a gas turbine, or the re-emergence of the high temperature liquid sodium reactor.

Noise

In many ways, the emission of noise is still the Achilles heel of the submarine, and the advent of nuclear propulsion has tended to make the problem worse with the achievement of higher speeds and the use of circulation pumps in the primary and secondary circuits. It is probably in this area of noise reduction that we can expect to see the greatest effort and improvement in the foreseeable future.

There is much that can be done. Detailed improvements to pump design and the hydraulic resistance of the core and heat transfer circuits enable both the pump power and the number of pumps to be reduced; raising the steam generators in the hull relative to the reactor core enables a measure of natural circulation to take place which further reduces — or even eliminates — the need for pump power. The latter measure is difficult to achieve in the limited space of a submarine hull, but all of these techniques have been applied to some of the more recent submarines in service.

The entire secondary machinery can be insulated from the hull by noise-suppressing mountings, and the use of noise reducing tiles on the hull itself can make further substantial reductions in the noise signature. Perhaps the most exciting development of all will be the use of 'anti-noise' vibrations, generated by transponders fixed to the hull which can be tuned to cancel all emitted noise over some range of speed. The nuclear submarine has enough power available to drive devices of this kind, and there is little doubt that the next decade will see the commissioning of submarines which are, perhaps, a hundred times quieter than their forbears (Fig 6).

Diving depth

The ability to dive deep has always been a feature which has assisted the submarine to escape detection, and even though the advent of the nuclear depth-charge has reduced the value of this manoeuvre, it is to be expected that developments in this area of performance will continue. The pressure hull is the major component of weight in a submarine, so that we must look to the development of new materials to effect

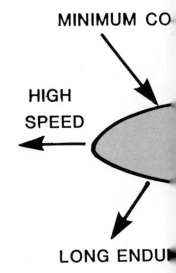

Figure 4. The factors affecting nuclear design

Drag, noise and heat problems arising from doubling the speed

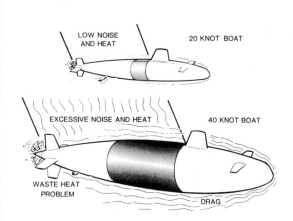

Noise reduction methods

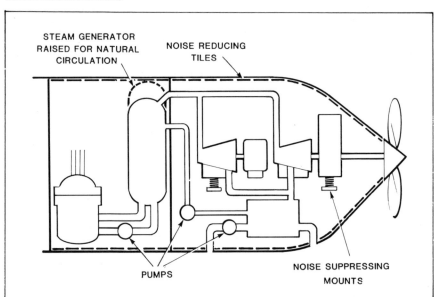

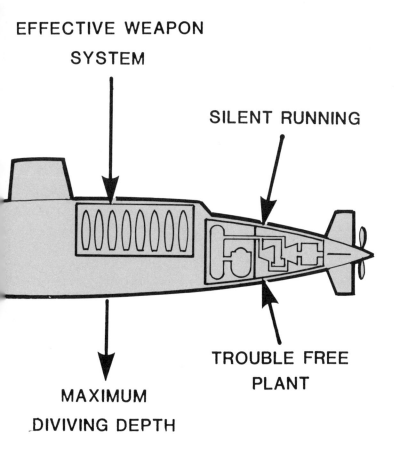

EFFECTIVE WEAPON
SYSTEM

SILENT RUNNING

MAXIMUM
DIIVING DEPTH

TROUBLE FREE
PLANT

substantial improvements without detraction of the submarine performance. Such materials must be able to survive the corrosive environment of the ocean, have subsequently better strength to weight ratio than steel and be capable of fabrication into pressure-tight structures. Titanium is a possible candidate, but the huge investment in manufacturing technology required to realise the potential of a new material in this exacting use will limit the development large, deep-diving submarines in the near future.

Summary

The adaption of the nuclear power plant for submarine use has already revolutionised the strategy and tactics of under-sea warfare. The nuclear submarine of today can maintain submerged speeds comparable to most surface ships, is limited in endurance only by the sustenance of the crew and is able to supply power to operate sophisticated navigation aids and powerful sonars. In the next decade, we may expect to see these vessels become much quieter, somewhat faster and develop longer range sonars and weapons (such as Harpoon), which will establish them as key strategic factors for world peace.

Early Russian submarines

● by Lieutenant Commander John M Maber, RN (Retired)

A BAVARIAN ARTILLERY corporal, William Bauer, driven by the impetus of war, in 1850 devised a submarine which, adequate financial support being forthcoming, was built at Kiel as the answer to the Danish blockade of the north German ports. *Der Brandtaucher* (alias *Sea Diver*) failed and, in the absence of further German interest, Bauer hawked his ideas around Europe until he reached Russia where he managed to convince the Grand Duke Constantine of the viability of his proposals for an improved submarine. Thus, his second boat, named *Le Diable-Marin* (alias *Sea Devil*) was laid down at the Leuchternberg Works at St Petersburg (Leningrad) in 1855 and was put afloat towards the

end of that same year. Some 54 feet long and propelled by a manually-driven screw, this second submarine proved reasonably successful and made many dives during the course of a variety of experiments off Kronstadt. Double bottom ballast tanks were filled to reduce buoyancy and the boat then dived through the action of a sliding weight, the adjustment of which forwards or aft could be used to control the inclination or trim of the craft. Although otherwise essentially simple Bauer's

boat incorporated an air lock enabling a diver to leave and re-enter to place mines or work on the sea bed. *Le Diable-Marin*, probably the first Russian submarine, came to grief off Ochda a year or two later and, despite an invitation to build another submarine, Bauer left the country whereupon the government quickly lost all interest in the subject.

In the wake of the departure of Bauer desultory experimental work continued but it was not until the Russian engineer, S Drzewiecki, turned his

attention in 1875 to the development of a practical submarine that any significant progress was made. His first boat, a 14 ft Odessa-built steel hulled craft, was driven by the action of a one-man crew working pedals to turn the screw, thus limiting the radius of action to that determined by the physical endurance of the man. As in the majority of submarines buoyancy was reduced by admitting water ballast, a state of equilibrium being maintained thereafter by the use of a small hand pump enabling water to be expelled or admitted as necessary. Compressed air provided the means for blowing ballast to bring the boat back to the surface.

The multi-purpose operator sat with his head in a glass dome and was provided with a pair of rubber sleeves and gloves secured to openings in line with his shoulders. By some unexplained means these sleeves were to be pressurised to match the external sea pressure and it was considered that the operator would then be able to insert his hands and arms thus by his own efforts to secure an explosive device to the hull of an enemy ship. It was not made clear as to how the operator was to control and manoeuvre his craft at the same time! The device was to be fired by the action of a clockwork mechanism.

Trials with this primitive craft at Odessa proved successful and stimulated the interest of the Russian Government to the extent that Drzewiecki was invited to develop the design for a larger, more sophisticated submarine capable of remaining submerged for several hours. Once again, however, the boat was to be man-propelled with a crew of four working

Drzewiecki submarine built in about 1880 and seen here at Vladivostok during the Russo-Japanese War 1904-1905, and shown right the Pyotr Koshka, pictured in about 1903, showing the two drop-collar 18-inch torpedo external fittings

two propellors via double pedals. The diving system copied that of the earlier craft but, as in Bauer's submarine, a sliding weight moved forwards or aft served to adjust trim, being controlled in this case by rod and chain gearing from the glass-windowed conning tower. Laid down at St Petersburg in 1879 the first submarine of this improved style, 19.5 ft long and of 8 ft maximum diameter (the hull being cigar-shaped) was completed in that same year and ran trials on Lake Gatschina where speeds of three to four knots were achieved with the submarine diving to 15 feet. The weapon load comprised a pair of buoyant mines, each charged with 110 pounds of dynamite, to be released beneath the intended victim and secured by spikes to the hull! The mines were detonated electrically from the parent craft.

Amongst other novel features the boat was fitted with a simple periscope (optical tube) although it is probable that it projected no more than a foot or two above the conning tower roof. Some such device was clearly essential in a

craft able to remain shut down for several hours, lying on the bottom if necessary since, obviously, the crew could sustain their propulsive effort for only a limited time. Compressed air could be bled into the boat to help maintain the quality of the atmosphere in addition to which a caustic soda scrubber was provided for the removal of carbon dioxide. Lifting points, forward and aft, were provided so that the boat might be hoisted aboard a parent craft for transport and maintenance.

Following a demonstration attended by the Minister of War, 50 single-screw, although otherwise similar, craft were ordered but they proved to have limited capabilities and few were completed for their intended role in harbour defence. However, one of this number was converted by Drzewiecki to battery-electric propulsion enabling the crew to be cut to two. The speed of four and a half to five knots and the limited endurance again suggested that the tiny craft was of doubtful utility but the adoption of an electric drive was in itself

a significant step in the development of the practical submarine as a fighting unit.

Thereafter Russian interest in the submarine waned once more although this was by no means the end of Drzewiecki's activities in the field. His early boats had been too small, underpowered and too slow; but in 1896 he was one of 29 participants in a competition organised by the French Ministry of Marine for a submarine of no more than 200 tons displacement, with a cruising range of 100 miles and speeds of 12 knots on the surface and eight knots submerged. Drzewiecki proposed a single screw boat of 190 tons displacement with steam machinery for an estimated speed in surface trim of 15 knots and storage battery/electric propulsion when submerged. More important was the proposed weapon fit consisting of two torpedoes stowed externally in Drzewiecki 'drop collars', one on either side of the boat, and secured by flexible steel bands. Once the firing sequence was initiated and the latter released, a pneumatic linkage

moved the torpedo out to a pre-set discharge angle capable of being varied, relative to the fore and aft line, from 10° off the bow to 160°. The final movement of the linkage unlatched and started the torpedo which moved off, provided the discharge angle had been accurately set, towards the intended target.

Drzewiecki's design, his most ambitious yet, won him second place in the competition but was soon forgotten although, on the other hand, his drop-collar system found favour and was adopted by both the French and, later, the Russian navies. The main drawback to this system was that the torpedo, carried externally, was subjected to full diving pressure while weed, flotsam and the effects of buffetting by the sea played havoc with the reliability of the weapon and its release mechanism. As for Drzewiecki himself, he was to reappear as the designer of a pair of larger submarines for the Russian navy in the wake of the Russo-Japanese War of 1904-05.

At the turn of the century the Russian Government evinced further interest in

35

submarine development. By now, pioneer work in the USA and France had brought the state of the art to a stage where the submarine was regarded as an integral part of the fleet, albeit for harbour defence only. Renewed Russian interest centred initially on a small submarine designed by Lieutenant Kolbassieff and Engineer Kuteinikoff which was put afloat at Kronstadt in 1901. The cigar-shaped *Matros Pyotr Koshka*, of 60 tons surface displacement, 50 feet long and of 14 feet maximum diameter, was powered by a combination of Bari-type storage batteries and electric motors driving twin screws for eight knots in surface trim and a reported six knots submerged. Two 18in Whitehead torpedoes were carried in Drzewiecki drop collars but, like earlier Russian submarines, the *Pyotr Koshka* was of doubtful potential, due to the limitations imposed by a reliance on storage batteries. By 1905 she

was serving with the Black Sea torpedo flotilla, apparently as its only submarine, being credited at that time with a radius of action of 20 miles and speeds of six knots on the surface and a low three and a half knots submerged according to *Janes Fighting Ships 1905-06*.

In 1903, at last, the problem of limited endurance was overcome by the adoption of an internal combustion engine for surface propulsion. Designed by Engineer Bubnov and launched at St Petersburg in that year the 175-ton *Delfin*, a 77 ft long boat with a maximum diameter of 14 ft, was fitted with a Panhard petrol engine of French manufacture giving a speed in surface trim of 11 knots. Submerged, an electric motor powered by a battery of 64 cells drove the single screw. The armament consisted of four 18in Whitehead torpedoes carried in the now familiar Drzewiecki drop collars.

Ballasting arrangements followed the

practice of the day. The *Delfin* proved successful in the course of her trials which involved a 36 hour run from Kronstadt to Bjoerkoe including a total of 26 hours dived. In the event it was the ballasting arrangements which contributed to the undoing of the *Delfin*. During a demonstration off Kronstadt on June 29, 1904, with a number of trainees on board, the boat was being trimmed down by admitting ballast while the conning tower hatch was still open. It seems probable that water was being taken in too quickly when the wash from a passing vessel swamped the open hatch and the submarine went to the bottom with the loss of 24 lives. Despite the mishap, however, six more boats of this early Bubnov type were built at St Petersburg for service with the Baltic and Siberian flotillas while the *Delfin* herself, refloated and overhauled, rejoined the fleet, apparently in Siberian waters based upon Vladivostock.

The Russian Government realised the potential of submarines in a harbour-defence role, able to strike unseen against a blockading enemy force and, following the outbreak of war with Japan in 1904, the navy turned to foreign submarine builders to help meet the need. Indigenous development had run its course, for the acceptance into service of American- and German-built boats brought new ideas and techniques which necessarily influenced future submarine design for the imperial service.

Delfin in about 1904 shortly before her accidental flooding — an occurrence which cost 21 lives

Submarines and the Soviet Union

DESPITE THE CONSIDERABLE attention paid to the principle of the submersible by the Imperial Russian Court of the late 19th century this interest was more idiosyncratic than effective. Certainly the fact that a group of musicians played patriotic music in Wilhelm Bauer's *Le Diable Marin* while submerged off Kronstadt at the time of the coronation of Tsar Alexander II in 1856 will probably remain unique in history but it did little to promote Bauer's sales campaign or the principles of underwater warfare. Much the same is true of the 1879 order for 50 pedal-driven submersibles to be built to the Drzewiecki design. Although the first 30 of this class were so ineffective that the remainder were cancelled the Russians decided a few years later, more or less on a whim, to buy a Nordenfelt-Garrett steam-driven submersible: it went aground *en route* to the purchasers but it is safe to say that the clumsy craft would never have been successful operationally. Undaunted by failures the Russian naval staff continued to show interest as new models of 'underwater boats' appeared in various foreign navies. At the beginning of this century they began a submarine building programme which, with occasional hiccups, has continued until the present day.

The reason for this digression lies in the content of this programme. From Bauer to the pedal-submersibles the Russians were thinking of future possibilities as they affected the defence

● by Captain John E Moore, RN (Retired) who joined submarines in 1943 and had five submarine commands. Latterly he was in charge of the Soviet naval section in DIS before retiring in 1972 at his own request, being dissatisfied with the use of intelligence and the RN ship-building programme. He has been editor of Jane's Fighting Ships since November, 1972 and has written and edited a number of books on naval subjects and makes frequent TV and radio appearances

of their country. From 1900 onwards, through the Japanese war and in the years leading up to 1914, they showed initiative and a power of innovation which outstripped most other naval powers. In 1906 they produced a diesel submarine, two years behind the French but between two and six years ahead of the British, the Americans and the Germans. In 1908 they laid down the first submersible specifically designed as a minelayer. But, despite this original approach the Russian submarine fleet in 1914 was only a quarter the size of the British force, then the largest in the world with 78 boats. In the ensuing three years the contribution of the Russian submarines towards the war against Germany was unimpressive to say the least.

In the aftermath of the Revolution the navy of the new Soviet state, the Red Fleet, received little governmental support. After 1919 numbers and

efficiency fell even further and it was not until 1926 that the first Soviet building programme was approved containing a higher proportion of submarines than surface ships. With a break in design experience of about ten years the first new Soviet classes relied heavily on foreign ideas — the *D*-boats on Italian plans and the *L* class on the British *L55* which had been salvaged in 1928. Later, the *Stalinets* class profited from German designers working in the USSR; but the Soviet naval architects were now returning to the innovative approach which had characterised their predecessors of 30 years before. The small *Malyutka* of about 160 tons and the heavily armed 1,400 ton *Katyusha* classes represented the two ends of the scale, very different from the other designs which were mostly in the 600 ton range. By the time that Germany invaded the Soviet Union in June, 1941 some 280 submarines of all types had been

Delta III (SSBN), 11,000 tons submerged carrying 16 SS-N-18 liquid fuelled missiles with a range of 3,500 - 4,300 n. miles and with three or seven MIRVs. Built at Severodvinsk, the first boats were completed in 1976

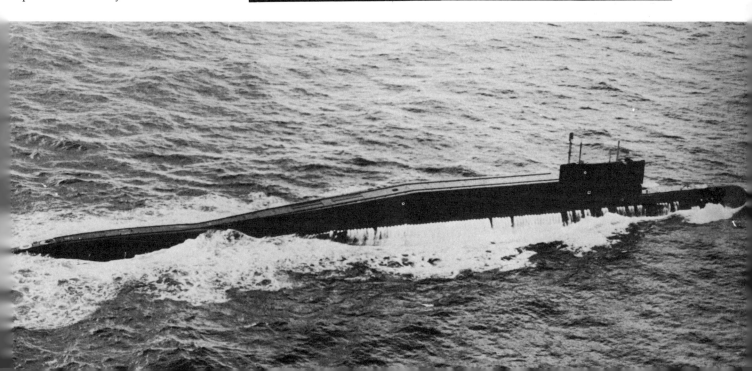

completed; but their contribution to the war again was unimpressive. Several of the commanding officers were brave and determined but the command structure had largely been demolished by Stalin's purges and the submariners lacked modern equipment.

In the immediate post-war period two revealing incidents underscored Soviet submarine problems. When the British boats on loan to the Soviet northern fleet were returned to the UK the ratings' messes had mostly been converted into officers' cabins — a gesture to the new socialism; and in one of the German Type VIIC U-boats handed over at Riga an astounded British officer watched while all the main working parts of the gyro compass were painted with Silverine. The old bywords in British boats that 'the man was all' and 'paint created more problems than it saved' were yet to be learned.

In July, 1945 Stalin ordered the rebuilding of the shattered Soviet fleet, a task made more difficult because of bombed Soviet shipyards and a design staff in disarray. But the capture of German technicians, scientists, submariners and equipment made that part of the task considerably easier. Added to this was the fact that the submarine building slips at Gorky and Komsomolsk had remained undamaged. Nevertheless, the massive building programme was daunting. More than 1,200 submarines were to be built between 1950 and 1965 at an initial rate of 78 a year rising to 100. The aim was to provide three zones of defence — 200 long-range boats (*Zulu* class and, later, *Foxtrots*), 900 medium-range boats (*Whiskey* class and, later, *Romeos*) and 100 short-range boats (*Quebec* class). Of these, some of the *Zulus* and *Quebecs* were fitted with Walter turbines or closed-cycle diesels but these were rendered unpopular by their frequent habit of bursting into flames — the infamous 'Cigar lighters'.

Two factors resulted in a change of course. After 28 out of the planned 40 *Zulus*, 60 out of 160 *Foxtrots*, 240 of the planned 340 *Whiskeys*, 20 of the 560 *Romeos* planned and 40 out of 100 *Quebecs* the back-wash of the post-Stalin defence reappraisal and the advent of nuclear power combined to change the entire building programme. Instead of the construction of torpedo-attack

submarines of the diesel-electric variety a whole series of variants began to appear to be identified as ballistic-missile (both nuclear and diesel propelled), cruise-missile with both types of propulsion and torpedo attack boats, both Fleet and Patrol. Thus by the late 1960s there were six varieties of submarine in the Soviet navy:

Ballistic-missile submarines (diesel propelled)

Early Soviet knowledge of ballistic-missile launching from submarines was founded entirely on German experience. Early trials by the Soviet navy were based on the V2(A4) missiles and the Lafferentz project in which V2 missiles were launched from capsules towed by U-boats. By September, 1955 the Soviet navy had turned to tube launchers and in that month the world's first SLBM launch from a submarine took place from a *Zulu V* class whose fin had been modified to take two tubes. Three years later the *Golf* class appeared with three tubes in the fin, still using the

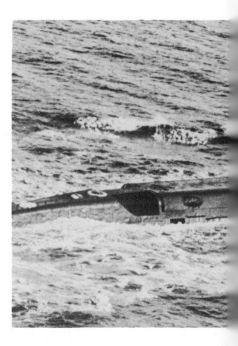

Artist's impression of the monster SSBN Typhoon launching one of its 20 missiles. It seems likely that the Soviet Navy regards the submarine as a mobile, submerged silo comparable, perhaps, to the mobile shore-based missile systems in the USA rather than as a traditional wide-ranging SSBN: it will probably remain in waters that are, in one way or another, protected, and on the right Echo II cruise-missile submarine (SSGN) carrying eight SS-N-12 or SS-N-3 missiles, and 20 torpedoes for the six 21-inch (533mm) tubes forward and two 16-inch (406mm) anti-submarine tubes aft. The anti-ship missiles have to be launched from the surface but with an estimated range of 550 Km (300 n.m.) this is tactically acceptable and this type of SSGN would pose a serious threat to surface forces in war

SS-N-4 missile with a 300 mile range and requiring a surface launch. Between 1961 and 1972 13 of this class were converted to carry the SS-N-5 missile with more than double the range of its predecessor. This group was renamed *Golf II* and was the last of this type of Soviet submarine. Eventually the *Golf* class was progressively paid off or converted although in 1983 there are still six based in the Baltic.

Ballistic-missile submarines (nuclear propelled)

As the *Golf* class was being completed in 1958-62 so were the nuclear propelled *Hotel* class. These had three launch tubes in the fin which were initially armed with SS-N-4 missiles, converting to SS-N-5 between 1962-70. This was a poor payload for a 5,500 ton submarine but in 1967 the first *Yankee* class was commissioned, a great advance. In a 9,500 ton hull were fitted 16 tubes for the 1,300 nautical mile SS-N-6 missile, the whole boat bearing a marked resemblance to the *Ethan-Allen* class of the USN. The first of the latter class had been laid down in 1959 allowing adequate time for the plans of both the US and the Soviet designs to be matched. Output of the *Yankees* took priority in the period around 1970 when up to eight of this class were completed each year. Between 1967 and 1974 34 *Yankees* were completed but in 1972 the first of the new *Delta I* class appeared. Although 500 tons larger than the *Yankees* these submarines carried only 12 missiles but these were of a totally new type, the SS-N-8. Their range of 4,200 nautical miles meant that the *Deltas* could operate close to their home bases in the Murmansk area and cover targets throughout Europe and much of North America. From the Sea of Ochotsk, Hawaii, to the Philippines, China and the majority of the Far East countries could be targetted. From 1972-77 18 of this class were built — in 1975-76 four *Delta II* class appeared, 1,000 tons larger at 11,000 tons and carrying 16 missiles. Towards the end of the 1970s the Mod 2 SS-N-8 was available — similar to the original in having only one re-entry vehicle but with a range of 4,900 nautical miles. As the last of the other two *Delta* classes were completing the first *Delta III* was commissioned. There was little outward change to the hull; what was

that within the outer casing there are two separate hulls. If the torpedo tubes in fact are in the bow, or are beam tubes at the forward end of the main fin, the concentration of armament in the front half would make a lot of sense. The missiles themselves, the SS-N-20, gave a considerable amount of trouble in their test flights which began in January, 1980 but these had been resolved by October 14, 1982 when a simultaneous launch of four missiles took place from the first of class. Using solid fuel their range is between 4,500 and 5,000 nautical miles, a minimal improvement (if any) on that of the SS-N-8 Mod 2. But the SS-N-20 has at least nine and possibly 12 MIRV heads, the advantage of solid fuel and, probably, an improved navigation system.

Typhoon's design raises a series of questions, the first of which concerns the huge target reflecting area which she presents. Although Soviet writings refer to the possibility of 25,000 ton boats with a speed of around 45 knots it is doubtful if *Typhoon* is capable of more than 30. If

Charlie I cruise-missile submarine (SSGN) carrying eight SS-N-7 anti-ship missiles which are launched submerged at a maximum range of 35 miles. Six 21-inch torpedo tubes and 18 torpedoes are also carried. Both missiles and torpedoes can have nuclear warheads and the Charlies are tactically extremely formidable with a top speed of 28 kts; and, above, Kilo diesel-electric patrol torpedo-attack submarine displacing about 3,000 tons. Little is known about this class which was first seen (in the Far East) in 1981 but its shape suggests high speed submerged and a deep-diving capability

different was the missile system. The 16 tubes carried SS-N-18 missiles, the first production run of liquid fuelled rockets with MIRV heads. Each of the three independently targetted vehicles is of 200 kilotons the whole having a range of 3,500 nautical miles. The Mod 1 missiles were soon followed by Mod II in which the use of a single head increased the range to 4,300 nautical miles. In the Mod 3 version the range has reverted to 3,500 nautical miles but the number of heads has increased to seven. With the first boat completed in 1976 14 more had been added by mid 1893 and series

production continues at Severodvinsk 402 yard.

In September 1980 the many rumours as to what to expect next were dissolved when the first *Typhoon* class was revealed. This giant amongst submarines was not only huge in size (nearly 560 ft long with a dived displacement around 30,000 tons) but was a turn-around in the placement of her missile tubes. Of these 20 are fitted forward of the fin with the forward hydroplanes set well in the bow. The flat-topped casing runs right aft to a large tail fin and there is a suggestion

this vast sonar target, proceeding at a comparatively modest speed by modern standards, is to operate beyond Soviet protected waters she must be at more than usual risk. Therefore it seems likely that her patrol area is in the northern seas and that her form is adequate to break through fairly thick ice. With modern communications at fairly short range this should not cause insurmountable problems. With the known Soviet capability in underwater signalling a second string to the instructional bow is possibly available.

Allowing for all this, why the gigantic size? The length of a protracted nuclear submarine's patrol is influenced more by the resilience of the ship's company than anything else. Allowing for Soviet methods of training and discipline it is probably not unreasonable to suggest 120 days, but this is unlikely to call for such a vast design. The ability to house two nuclear reactors in a submarine is standard Soviet practice in the bigger boats, so that idea is of little assistance. All the time the nagging question

remains, 'Why so big?' If the American *Ohio* class can carry 24 Trident missiles in the same length as *Typhoon* how come the latter carries four less missiles and is still about 11,000 tons greater dived displacement than *Ohio*? The answer may lie in the twin hull theory, a method of protection which, with the 13-15 ft separation between the outer and inner hulls, might be effective even against shaped-charge warheads or the concussion from a nuclear explosion in the sea.

Cruise missile submarines (diesel propelled)

Despite the advantages gained from German experience the Soviet navy lagged behind the USN in this sphere of submarine development. The latter had operated the Loon missile from submarines in 1948-49 and had embarked the Regulus, a strategic cruise-missile, soon afterwards. But after their first nuclear cruise-missile submarine had been completed in 1960 the USN, with Polaris now at sea,

Current Soviet Submarine Deployments (1983)

Type	FLEETS			
	Northern	Baltic	Black Sea	Pacific
SSBN	45	-	-	24
SSB	2	6	-	7
SSGN	28	5	-	20
SSG	8	-	1	4
SSN	40	23	22	22
SS*	55			50

*Plus about 85 in reserve

Papa cruise-missile submarine (SSGN) carrying anti-ship
missiles with a probable range of 70 miles. With two nuclear
reactors and two shafts this lone submarine of the class
has a top speed around 35 kts. The two shafts may be intended
to limit the effects of possible damage in or under the ice-cap

abandoned this approach.

Not so the Soviet navy. After the end
of the Korean war in 1953 had released
large numbers of Western aircraft
carriers, many with the capability of
carrying aircraft loaded with nuclear
weapons, Soviet plans were laid for a
possible riposte. The *Whiskey* class was
selected as the submarine carrier but it
seems more likely that those which were
converted to carry the SS-N-3 missiles
were intended for shore bombardment.
These missiles had a range of about 400
miles and would have needed external
guidance for ship attacks. At this stage
(1958-60) *Bear* and *Badger* aircraft were
entering service but, contrary to some
firm statements, it seems more likely
that these early SSBs were designed for
a tit-for-tat role against shore targets,
there being little evidence of much
experience in aircraft control.

Between 1960-68 the 16 *Juliett* class

were built at Gorky. These submarines,
though still having to launch their four
SS-N-3A on the surface carried mid-
course guidance radars in the fin and
were thus of a configuration adequate
for engaging ship targets. They were
also the last diesel propelled cruise
missile boats.

Cruise missile submarines
(nuclear propelled)

Concurrently with the start of the *Juliett*
programme five boats of the *Echo I* class
were built at Komsomolsk. These had
six SS-N-3 launchers in the after casing
on a hull similar to the first nuclear
attack submarines of the *November* class,
though 14 ft longer. This was an interim
class, all five having their missile tubes
removed between 1969-74. The absence
of mid-course guidance radars suggests
that *Echo I* may have had more of a
strategic than a tactical role, becoming

redundant as the *Yankee* class became available.

The *Echo II* class was completed between 1961-67 possibly making use of nuclear building capacity made available by the break between the *Hotel* and *Yankee* classes construction. Twenty nine were built and had the same guidance radars as *Juliett,* were 10 ft longer than *Echo I* and carried eight launchers. All remain in service in 1983 although six have been modified to launch SS-N-12 missiles with a range of 270 nautical miles instead of 180 nautical miles for the SS-N-3.

1967 was a vintage year for new Soviet classes — not only did it see new classes of surface ships and the *Yankees* but also the externally similar *Charlie I* cruise missile boats and the *Victor I*

SSNs. The latter two were of a new generation; both classes had shorter hulls with greater beam as well as a new nuclear propulsion system. But the greatest difference was in the *Charlies'* missiles. They carry eight tubes built in either side of the bow which house SS-N-7 missiles. Not only were these the first semi-vertical launch tubes in any navy but the missiles, with a range of 37 nautical miles, were the first capable of underwater launch. The whole system made sense only if there were an organic missile control system.

In 1972 came the first *Charlie II,* 30 ft longer with the same number of tubes as the preceding class but armed with SS-N-9 missiles with a range of 60 nautical miles. The increased range probably required improved targetting facilities

but the increase in length was almost certainly due to the introduction of the SS-N-15, a Subroc type weapon launched from the six 21 in torpedo tubes. By 1980 six *Charlie II* class had been completed. In 1971 the single *Papa* class had appeared, 20 ft longer than *Charlie II* was to be and with a different shape for her missile tube covers. There were ten tubes, the fin was more angular and the casing higher than in *Charlie I.* Expectations of a considerable number of this new design were, however, unfounded, *Papa* remained a loner carrying SS-N-9 missiles and being, possibly, the trials submarine for the next stage of development.

As the *Charlie II* programme came to an end in 1980 the first of the *Oscar* class was launched at Severodvinsk. This design really was a brain-shaker for NATO staffs. In a hull of 460 feet with a dived displacement of about 14,000 tons she carries 24 missile tubes housing the 270 nautical mile SS-N-19. Twin screws, as in *Papa,* give her a speed of about 35 knots which is exceptional for a submarine with a beam of about 60 ft. Once again the Soviet navy has produced a giant but in this case the need for size is apparent — the missile tubes are placed down either side of an

Victor II fleet submarine (SSN) with two nuclear reactors and one shaft giving a top speed of about 31 kts. The diving depth is estimated at 2,000 ft (600m) and the armament includes the SS-N-15 anti-submarine missile, launched from submerged, which releases a nuclear depth charge over the target at ranges out to 35 miles

One of about six Alfa fleet submarines with titanium alloy hulls for deep diving (about 2,000 ft or 600m) and a very high speed of 42 kts. Anti-submarine missiles (SS-N-15), torpedoes and/or mines can be embarked

enormous fin, let into the outer casing and occupying a good third of the total length.

The possession of this submarine and the follow-on members of the class is of considerable importance to Soviet planners. With a maximum closing speed on a NATO battle-group of some 70 knots, updated missile control and satellite intelligence, this class presents a formidable threat of a totally different order from that of the *Charlies*.

Patrol submarines

Of the 1,200 non-nuclear submarines originally planned for in 1948 only 388 were built. The term 'non-nuclear' is used as a number of the *Zulu* and *Quebec* classes were built with either Walter turbines using high-test peroxide (HTP) or closed cycle diesels. The Soviet navy had the same problems as the British with HTP. All the boats so fitted were converted to diesel-electric although there is evidence of continuing Soviet interest in unconventional methods of propulsion. This may well include a maritime application of the British-invented fuel cell.

The follow-on class after the original *Zulus, Whiskeys, Romeos* and *Quebecs* was the successful *Foxtrot* class. The first was completed in 1958 and the last, No 62, intended for Soviet use was commissioned in 1971. Since then new construction has continued for client countries — two for Cuba, eight for India and five for Libya.

The first of the *Tango* class appeared at the Sebastopol naval review in July, 1973. Of about the same length as the *Foxtrots* these submarines are more than three feet wider in the beam with an increase to 3,700 tons dived

displacement. In a continuing programme of two per year a total of 20 will be in commission by late 1983. Their role must include operations in the considerable shallow water area around the USSR and in these tasks they have now been joined by five boats of the new *Kilo* class. The first of these was completed at Komsomolsk in 1979 and building continues at that yard at a rate of about one per year. Shorter by 72 ft than the *Tango* class (229.6 ft compared with 301.8 ft.) they have the same 29.5 ft beam with a dived displacement of 3,200 tons. These variations in design are presumably necessary but the reasons are not immediately evident.

Fleet submarines

From 1950 development of marine nuclear propulsion advanced rapidly in the USSR. By 1953 the building of the first reactor was underway and in 1958 the first Soviet nuclear propelled submarine was completed. This was the

first of 14 *November* class with two reactors, two turbines and two shafts. They were 360 ft long with a remarkable beam/length ratio of 1:12, very similar to the *Hotel* and *Echo I* classes. Basically all three were of the interesting *Shark* design, very long and comparatively slender but in 1967 the arrival of the *Victor I* class showed a new concept in both hull design and propulsion. By 1974 16 had been built at Admiralty Yard and Gorky. At 5,200 tons dived displacement they were slightly more than the *Novembers* but on a length of 308 ft their beam/length ratio dropped to 1:9.4. Before the *Victor I* programme was completed *Victor II* appeared in 1972. Built at the same yards as their predecessors seven were completed by 1978. They were 20 ft longer, an addition which may have been necessitated by the inclusion of SS-N-15 in their armament. As the *Victor II* run came to an end in 1978 a vigorous construction programme at Leningrad and Komsom-

44

olsk began to produce the *Victor III*. In the intervening five years 16 of the submarines have been completed. They are 13 ft longer than *Victor II* but all three marks have the same propulsion system of two reactors, two turbines geared to a single shaft with the addition of two auxiliary propellers. The operational depth of the *Victors* is around 1,300 ft with a crushing depth of 2,000 ft. The major difference between *Victor III* and her predecessors is the addition of a large pod mounted on the after fin probably the first operation deployment of a 30 ft fixed sonar array in the Soviet submarine fleet. It is also reported that the whole hull and fin are coated with Chester Guard anechoic covering.

While the various *Victors* were logical improvements on each other and previous designs, a totally different concept was realised in the *Alfa* class. The original interest in this submarine was that the first was laid down in the mid 1960's, requiring a design effort

beginning in 1960-61 at the latest. At this time the British had been forced to take an American reactor for *Dreadnought* and the first Soviet *November* class had been in commission for only two or three years. Originality and innovation were evident in all aspects of this class. Just over 80 ft shorter than *Victor III* but with the same beam, her dived displacement of 3,800 tons is 2,200 tons less and similar to that of the *Tango* class. The beam/length ratio dropped to 1:7.9. This was a fascinating departure in view of the *November* class building being concurrent with the *Alfa* design and the fact that the *Victor* group increased to 1:10. But other more startling advances were to come to light. With a titanium alloy hull the operational diving depth was increased to about 3,000 ft and the speed of at least 42 knots was a radical increase beyond anything then planned in the west. The ship's company had been markedly reduced to 60 or less and of this total only a very few were not

experienced senior ratings and officers.

All this improvement was achieved only during a long period of trials and evaluation. The first submarine was completed at Sudomekh yard, Leningrad in 1970 after some five years on the slip. By 1974 she had been dismantled and it was not until 1976 that the second boat was completed. Since then one *Alfa* has been completed about every 15 months. The question now is whether this is a truly operational class or a series of research and development submarines. The cost of such a boat must be an important factor here. The production of titanium itself, despite the large reserves of ore in the USSR, is an extremely expensive performance and the shaping and welding of the necessary components of a pressure hull is a matter of very high technology. The chances would seem reasonable that the *Alfas* are primarily high performance test vehicles with a considerable potential as attack submarines, particularly as part of

a screen defending the Soviet SSBN operating areas. The probability of the successor to both the *Alfa* and *Victor III*, a comparatively small, deep diving and very fast submarine, being in commission by late 1984 seems high.

Specialised submarines

Some of the elderly diesel submarines have been converted to serve as research submarines for various organisations such as Fisheries. In addition to these large boats a considerable number of small and very small submarines has been developed, apparently for research of various kinds. A further expansion of this variety of underwater craft is the Deep Submergence Recovery Vehicle, DSRV. Recently the *India* class submarine of 4,800 tons dived displacement appeared, a rescue submarine with two DSRVs carried in the after casing.

About the same time as the first *India* appeared the single *Lima* class was completed by the Sudomekh Yard, Leningrad in 1979. The outward shape suggests that *Lima* is designed for hydro-acoustic trials and so far only one has been seen. But the third specialised design, the *Bravo* class, has four members deployed in the North, Pacific and Black Sea Fleets. These hump-backed boats, the first of which was completed in Komsomolsk in 1968, presented a profile familiar to the more elderly British submarines who remembered the Padded-*S* class of some 30 years ago. These are boats with the same task, to act as targets for ASW and torpedo exercises.

Armament

Apart from the missile armament of the ballistic and cruise missile submarines already mentioned, all Soviet operational submarines are fitted with at least six 21 in torpedo tubes. Unclassified information on the torpedoes themselves is scanty but some aspects are well-documented. Long-range torpedoes, probably similar to the later marks of the US Type 48, are available and the use of nuclear heads is certain. Wire guidance has been in use for a long time and weapon control has probably benefitted from extensive Soviet industrial espionage in the USA.

Other torpedoes have been available over the years, particularly the 16 in anti-submarine weapon for which special tubes were fitted in many of the earlier nuclear and diesel submarines. In addition any Soviet submarine has a mine-laying capability, an aspect which must always be remembered since the

Bravo padded target diesel-electric submarine. One is allocated to each fleet for anti-submarine weapon-firing exercises

USSR today has the world's largest stockpile of mines of all types. These include the AMD 1000 with magnetic pressure, acoustic or combination variants, rising mines such as Cluster Bay and Cluster Gulf and nuclear mines of up to 20 kilotons.

In the late 1960s or early 1970s a new weapon was added to the inventory, the SS-N-15. This is similar to the American Subroc giving a much longer range capability than before. A nuclear head is probably incorporated in this weapon.

Navigation

On the last occasion on which a Soviet ship made a passage to the North Pole it was stated that at least seven satellites had provided navigation and communications assistance. There is no doubt that amongst the plethora of Soviet space-craft, there are many to be utilised for both these purposes. However the linkage between satellite navigation and a form of Ships Inertial Navigation System (SINS) is not clear, although there is little doubt that both methods have benefited from' information obtained from western technology.

Communications

In the late 1960s the Soviet submariners were struggling to produce adequate floating aerials but this problem has, apparently, been overcome. While the US Navy was being hard-pressed by the environmental lobby over the introduction of ELF stations, the Soviet Navy went ahead and today a large number of their submarines are fitted with ELF, VLF and the more normal VHF and SHF methods of communication. Floating aerials and communications buoys are now common-place and the ability to communicate with SSBNs under ice is certain.

Conclusion

Two factors have provided the Soviet submarine fleet in 1983 with powerful advantages: continuity in design and the far higher proportion of GNP spent on research and development than in western countries. At the same time, however, there is a notable lag in some particular areas of high technology to which the Soviets will be directing their future espionage activities. Improvements in the targetting accuracy of submarine-launched ballistic missiles and in the use of solid propellants for these weapons, calibration software algorithms, inertial navigation systems, acoustic sensor technology, particularly as applied to towed arrays, signal processing hardware and software, submarine quieting and computer improvements probably rank at the top of the list.

History suggests that the Soviet method is to solve one major problem at a time. For instance, speed was necessary in nuclear submarines; this was achieved by pushing great power into the water, accepting the noise penalty. Having achieved the speed the next problem is to suppress the noise. Innovation by steps is a Soviet characteristic which has allowed great advances to be made in certain directions. The western method of attempting to solve all the problems before starting on a prototype may have some advantages but one of these is not rapid and continued evolution.

Bootle's Christmas Party

● by Richard Compton-Hall

CHRISTMAS WAS approaching fast. But the nuclear deterrent multi-megaton Polaris submarines squatting heavily in the water at the Clyde Submarine Base were not looking particularly festive. Merriment was minimal. Some of the older Chief Petty Officers — the technicians especially — openly admitted that they believed in Santa Claus no more. Rumours from their American opposite numbers up the way at Holy Loch suggested that the USN had also become sceptical. True, Christmas cards had started to arrive from the French Force de Frappe but they lacked the innocent childish fun that goes with Christmas stockings, white beards and reindeer. And there were absolutely no greetings at all from the Soviet SSBN submariners — which was sad, seeing that they lived closer to fantasy and Father Christmas than anybody else.

Even the most dedicated of nuclear deterrers can know depression in the depths of darkest Scotland in December — especially when many of their non-nuclear brethren are known to be living it up as far south as Charleston, Carolina and the Isle of Wight.

The Captain (S/M) Tenth Submarine Squadron took stock and sighed. He had not been asked down for a duty-free drink in a submarine since a rather formal occasion (negative the hard stuff) on the Queen's official birthday. His men had forgotten what real submarining was. The megatons were getting on their minds. What they needed was new blood. He reached for a signal pad.

The new blood duly arrived in the crudest of fossil-fuelled vehicles — a diesel submarine packed to the heaving brim with a loud, cheerful and resolutely conventional Ship's Company. They took over the nuclear base and its amenities with the ravenous ease of 64 perambulating locusts, including one elderly and noticeably stunted locust, identified eventually as Leading Stoker Bootle.

Captain S/M 10 greeted the Ship's Company of HMS Unbridled, forgetting that conventional submarine psychology was of an earthier, oilier kind. 'Nice to have a good old-fashioned boat up here. Don't worry if you can't understand what all these nuclear chaps are talking about. Just join in — jolly things along a bit — do the best you can.

And a Very Merry Christmas to you all.' 'Many Happy Megatons to you too, mate,' muttered Unbridled's Chief Stoker. It summed up the meeting's general mood.

That evening the Unbridled Stoker's Mess en bloc assembled a quantity of flares and small arms ammunition on the submarine's casing while Captain S/M dined some local notables in the wardroom ashore. As the port passed for the second time a series of detonations rent the cultured conversation and orange flashes lit the sky.

Burdened with alarm, despondency and curried eggs, Captain S/M and his guests raced to the jetty where they were able to enjoy a rendering, forte, to the tune of John Brown's Body:
'We're deterring Father Christmas and he won't come down tonight.
'We're . . . etc. (The etceteras were, fortunately, blurred by the alarm sirens which, ever alert, the base guardians had set off more in hope than anger).

Captain S/M realised the extent of the problem almost immediately. He, after all, had done the Staff Course and this was not what he had meant by 'jollying things along a bit.' It jolly well wasn't cricket.

Diversionary tactics were clearly required as recommended by the Staff

The children advanced steadily up the gangway with implacable menace

Manual. A children's party — that would do the trick, bright little faces carolling midst the missiles. A lovely thought and the non-nuclear submariners could run the party, a *splendid* way of melding the matelots.

While the more knowing members of *Unbridled*'s Ship's Company took to the woods Bootle was engaged in disconnecting a polished copper pressure gauge from No 3 main boiler in the base heating plant. His quiet but triumphant return was marred by the discovery that he, alone out of countless volunteers, had been elected as Duty Leading Hand on the day of the Party.

The children advanced steadily up the gangway with implacable menace, led by the notorious Honourable Hamish — heir to Lord McSporren-the-Damned — from the Castle up the Glen. The Honourable Hamish was frankly disappointed.

'I thought it'd be the Captain,' he complained.

'Season's greetings,' growled Bootle and handed over a rubber-coated wheelspanner — one of several Christmas presents he had garnered for the occasion from the Chief Stoker's Store.

'I want to play with the reactor,'

' 'Aven't got one. Can't do that,' growled Bootle.

'What *can* you do them?' demanded the juvenile McSporran.

'Anything,' Bootle snarled.

In silence he led the children below where he had made a variety of entertainment — at a price. Wearing the absent First Lieutenant's sea-going uniform was charged at whatever Bootle judged an infant Scotsman would be able to afford. A look at the Chief Stoker's photograph album (children under ten not admitted) was more expensive. But these and other diversions soon palled. Something small and very Scottish tugged at Bootle's sleeve.

'I want to see an aeroplane,' it said.

The Hon Hamish backed it up,

'You *said* you could do *anything*.'

Bootle looked steadily at his tormentors. It was about time them neutrons in the big boats did a bit to help. He wandered casually up onto the casing and waved to the sentry on the Polaris submarine astern.

'One of your lads doin' a bit of divin' then?' he asked conversationally. 'No? Then I must 'ave bin imaginin' that black

'elmet I saw swimmin' round your stern.'

The nuclear base went to Action Stations with commendable speed. Bootle summoned his guests up top.

'You wanted an aeroplane,' he said, 'it should be 'ere about . . . *now*.'

At that moment a helicopter hopped obligingly over the hill and hovered noisily over the water, searching for intruders. Meanwhile the base uncovered anti-aircraft missiles, telephoned the Prime Minister and issued all nuclear submariners with tin hats and gas-masks. Royal Marines and SAS men, with blackened faces and machine guns, poured out of hidden bastions; frogmen leaped into the water; and motor boats busily buzzed up and down dropping scare-charges.

Bootle encountered Captain S/M the next day.

'I hear the party was a great success,' said Captain S/M. 'Sorry I didn't have a chance to see the children myself. I was, er, rather busy. What exactly did you do?

'Just did me best sir. Jollyin' things along and that,' said Bootle vaguely. 'I spec it was gettin' everyone to join in wot did it . . .'

Tomato problems

TEMPORARILY WE WERE carrying a doctor. This was unusual; in the days before nuclear reactors, which need the constant attention of medical practitioners, submariners were subjected to the ministrations of the Captain and the Coxswain with maybe a helping hand from the First Lieutenant if he wasn't otherwise occupied. These experts were guided by an invaluable blood-red publication titled *The Small Ship's Medical Handbook*, written in simple language in nice big type. Starting, perhaps, at 'Stomach, bottom right-hand corner, pain in' one could follow the symptoms through to the most exciting conclusions. It was disappointing, though, that, at the end of every trail, one came

● by Richard Compton-Hall

up hard against a stop sign: 'Give no treatment, turn the patient in, and reassure him. *Give no alcohol*.'

With a real doctor on board we hoped for better things and eagerly looked forward to the outbreak of some disastrous disease. But unfortunately the doctor was a keen amateur gardener and could talk of little else. It looked like being a strictly horticultural voyage.

As luck would have it, however, we were not to be entirely disappointed. On the third day out one of the fore-

endmen shuffled uneasily into the wardroom to report he was 'suffering discomfort'. The nature of the discomfort was explained in confidential whispers behind the wine-locker where the Navigator usually sat. It was the best that could be done by way of a private surgery.

'Let's have a look then,' we heard the doctor say as we averted our eyes uneasily. There was a pause. I remember that the Torpedo Officer hummed a bar or two from Iolanthe. One's consciousness is sharpened at moments like this. Then, loud and clear, our doctor made his pronouncement, 'If you were a tomato, lad, I'd say you had blossom-end rot . . .'

Type 2400 — a new patrol class submarine

● By Bill Clouter, **Public Relations Manager for Vickers Shipbuilding and Engineering Ltd**

AS NUCLEAR-POWERED submarines (SSNs) began to join the Royal Navy in the 1960s the British Fleet planners inclined to the view that the successful *Oberon* class of conventional or diesel-electric submarines (SSKs) — which had just come into service — would be the last of their kind. All future boats would be nuclear-powered, since the operational advantages of the SSN — the 'true submarine' capable of operating indefinitely under water — were so marked.

However, the use of nuclear power in submarines involves large displacements, high capital and through-life costs and heavy demands, of course, on training, support and logistic facilities. Operational experience showed that the SSK, in addition to being much cheaper to build, man, operate and maintain, had the advantages of being more silent running and more suited to use in shallow waters. Although the SSK lacks the submerged speed endurance of the SSN it is better suited for surveillance/reconnaisance duties and in the important context of training the SSK provides better, more demanding target simulation for ASW forces generally.

It became evident that the nuclear submarine and its diesel-electric counterpart had complementary roles to play in the navy, both for peacetime tasks and in the event of war. Excellent though the *Oberon* had proved to be, the design was that of the early 1950s and although it had been updated there had been many developments in submarine technology. With these facts in mind, in the mid-70s an Outline Staff Requirement was drafted for a new SSK for the RN. During this period Vickers Shipbuilding and Engineering Limited (VSEL), who were collaborating with the Ministry of Defence in the on-going SSN programme, had continued to develop their range of diesel-electric submarines for export, and built six SSKs (including three *Oberons* for Brazil) for overseas customers. Operational requirements of the world's navies vary widely, but market assessments indicated that navies with long coast lines to patrol, or who needed a full ocean-going capability, would require a new, larger class of SSK.

From discussion and increasingly close collaboration between the Ministry and Vickers (as a part of British Shipbuilders since nationalisation in 1977) the Type 2400 design has emerged.

The boat has a submerged displacement of 2400 tonnes — as the *Oberon*. It is not merely an up-dated *Oberon* but a new class of diesel-electric submarine designed to meet RN requirements for several decades to come. Vickers, with Government approval offers variants of that design to meet the operational requirements of overseas navies including Australia and Canada. Certain design differences are inevitable — where practical, alternative machinery, equipment, weapons and sensors to meet the potential customer's particular requirement will be considered, but there are advantages in keeping the RN and export variants as similar as possible.

As collaboration and co-ordination has developed so has there been more delegation of responsibility to industry by the Ministry. Responsibility for design development has been handed over to Vickers, who have also been awarded the contract as Weapons Co-ordinating and System Design

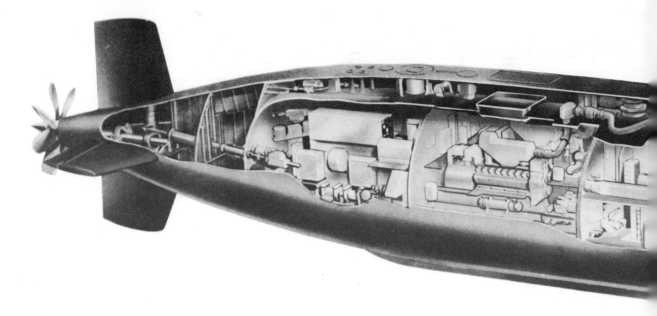

Authority. Included in the contract is the construction at Barrow of a comprehensive Shore Development Facility, progress on which is now well advanced.

The hull of the 2400

Modern detection techniques and associated weaponry dictate that a submarine must avoid surface running by carrying out transits and patrols either snorting or submerged. Contemporary hulls, therefore, are designed for optimum performance under water. The adoption of single skinned hulls with a high beam-to-length ratio enables good manoeuvre-ability and facilitates two or more decks, ie more useful deck area.

The pressure hull is made from high tensile steel of circular section, stiffened by internal high tensile steel frames. The forward and aft ends of the pressure hull end in dome bulkheads, as shown. The forward and aft external structure is constructed from high quality steel, except for the forward portion adjacent to the sonar array, which is of GRP. The structure houses the four main ballast tanks and various other items eg, the water transfer tank and the external portions of the torpedo tubes. Aft, a similar pattern pertains.

The bridge fin is made of GRP on a steel support structure. Of streamlined form it houses the masts, periscope upper bearings etc, as well as providing a forward navigation position. A steel keel extends the full length of the pressure hull. Its primary purpose is to provide a flat surface for operational bottoming and docking, but it also gives easily accessible stowage space for growth and stability ballast.

Internal arrangements

Within the pressure hull the space is divided into three main watertight compartments by two transverse bulkheads. In the two forward compartments there is a two-deck arrangement, the aft compartment having a single deck. The allocation of those spaces is shown in the diagram.

Three hatches give external access to the forward compartment, for torpedo embarkation, battery loading (and general access) and the third forms part of the forward escape position. The No 1 deck level of the compartment is the torpedo stowage space, with the six torpedo tubes penetrating the forward dome bulkhead. Stowage is provided for 12 21 in reload torpedoes. The No 2 deck level contains accommodation, the sonar console space and torpedo tube

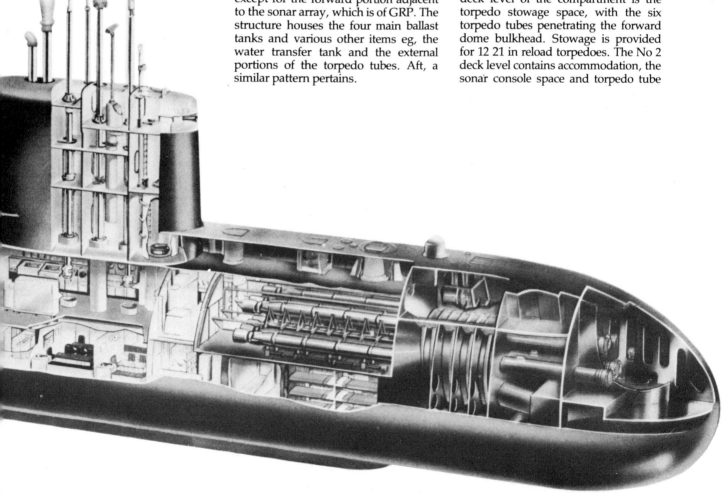

operating equipment. Most of the space below that deck is occupied by the forward battery compartment.

The No 1 deck level of the centre section houses the Control Room, Communications and ESM offices and the Commanding officers cabin. Two hatches give external access — one forward leads into the five-man escape chamber in the fin (shown in the diagram) and provides access to the navigation position. The other hatch, at the rear of the compartment, is the primary personnel access hatch and is also used for battery loading. No 2 deck level provides the auxiliary machinery space and a continuation of the forward accommodation spaces. Below this deck is the aft battery compartment and various tank installations.

The aft compartment houses the main and ancillary machinery and air conditioning units. The space is divided by an acoustic/thermal bulkhead — the main propulsion motor room aft and the engine room as the forward part, with oil storage beneath.

An important feature is the provision of a main machinery shipping opening in the pressure hull above the engine room large enough to enable diesel engine removal with minimum dismantling. The engine room serves as the aft escape compartment, with a one-man escape tower located in the propulsion motor room.

The lock-out chamber, already mentioned, is provided for use by divers when the boat is submerged. Inflatable dinghies and other equipment can be carried in a streamlined container attachable to the superstructure just behind the bridge fin. DSRV docking seats are fitted round the escape hatches of the two escape towers.

Complement and accommodation

Crew numbers have a significant bearing on through-life and training costs, and by full attention to ergonomics, automation in machinery spaces and integrated fire-control, substantial reductions in their numbers

have been achieved. The normal complement is seven officers, 13 senior ratings and 24 junior ratings — a total of 44, compared with *Oberon's* 68.

Accommodation is provided for a maximum of 46 and by submarine standards is of a high order. Every officer and rating is provided with his own bunk and personal stowage space, and, separate from the sleeping quarters, the wardroom, senior and junior ratings messrooms provide reasonable eating and off-duty facilities.

Machinery and power supplies

The single, fixed-pitch propeller is driven by a twin-armature electric motor sited in the aft section of the pressure hull and separated from the diesel generators in the engine room by the thermal/acoustic bulkhead. Propulsion power is provided by two separate battery banks charged by the diesel generators.

There are two high-speed 16-cylinder

Mrs Smith at home

● The world-wide proliferation of motels, except in the Soviet bloc where there must still be problems, has made it a good deal easier for submariners to cement friendships with local citizens of the opposite sex when visiting ports at home and abroad. A few years ago, however, liaisons were fraught with difficulties as this sad story shows

SUBMARINERS, BEING more than usually modest when ashore, sometimes adopt a nom-de-plume when circumstances suggest that anonymity is desirable. Certain pieces of submarine equipment lend themselves rather well to such pseudonyms! Mr Q Kingston, Mr H P Blow, Mr R D Test-Cock, for instance, can be found in hotel registers around the world.

But one young officer, new to the underwater service, scorned such common usage. When his time came, as come it does to all submariners sooner rather than later, he led the lady of his choice to the reception desk of a certain hotel in Glasgow and signed the book

with a flourish — Mr and Mrs Smith. The receptionist said not a word; matters proceeded as planned, and the lady discreetly slipped out of bed and hotel at daybreak.

Calling for his bill the young officer was shattered to find it amounted to £558 which seemed a trifle high for a single night of rest and relaxation.

Despite his abundant juniority the young officer took a stand and protested.

'Ah, Mr Smith,' said the clerk, 'it is true you were in the room for one night only. The charge for that's a wee six pounds. But, you see, Mrs Smith — she's been staying here on and off f[or] three months . . .'

mechanically supercharged diesel engines each coupled to an AC generator of approximately 1.25 MW output. The generators have in-built rectification providing the electrical power for charging the batteries when snorting or on the surface. Noise and shock attenuation is achieved by supporting the sets on resilient mountings.

The electrical systems may be considered as two parts, which share common battery and charging arrangements. One part is primarily concerned with propulsion and one with auxiliary and weapon services. The supply systems are at battery voltage, at 440V 60Hz, three-phase and single-phase, and at 24Vdc. Supplies are configured to provide high integrity, and dedicated supplies are provided where this is considered necessary.

Control and instrumentation

The need to reduce manpower, and progress in remote control, indication and monitoring techniques, have resulted in the incorporation of significant improvements in ship and machinery control and instrumentation.

Remote control for most, and monitoring of all, ship and machinery control systems is centralised, the main aims being to reduce the watchkeeping effort to the minimum, to ensure efficiency and safety in the control systems, and to produce ergonomically-designed control console arrangements — so as to co-ordinate ship and propulsion control, minimise operational error, and enable all ship and emergency operating procedures to be conducted safely and efficiently. In the event of remote control and/or monitoring failure, sufficent local instrumentation and controls are provided to enable safe plant operation, using additional watchkeepers if necessary.

A comprehensive monitoring system, essential to centralised control, is fitted which includes an efficent alarm annunciation and warning capability. Parameters directly associated with plant and submarine safety are monitored by the 'hardwired' alarm system. Each channel consists of a sensor directly connected to a dedicated alarm indicator and a common audible warning. If a hardwired alarm is initiated, immediate remedial action is required by the ship's company.

Less important parameters are monitored by a second-level surveillance system whose failure will not endanger the safe operation of machinery or the submarine.

Weapons and sensors

Standard armament provides an effective weapons payload complemented by a sophisticated sensor kit. The six weapon tubes are capable of accommodating a range of 21in diameter weapons, including dual-purpose wire-guided heavyweight torpedoes, anti-ship air-flight guided missiles and submarine mines.

Depending on the weapons mix the forward magazine space will accommodate up to 12 full-length reloads borne on special shock-mounted pallets; an associated handling system permits rapid reloading.

The low noise-emission qualities of the Type 2400 make it an excellent sonar platform. The sonar suite provides long-range passive detection and analysis, using hull-mounted, passive, active and intercept sonars; passive bow sonar, capable of simultaneous LF and HF band operation, with adaptive processing channels to provide good target discrimination under adverse conditions. Simultaneous automatic tracking of several targets is possible with digital data transfer to the Action Information Organisation (AIO).

The attack and search periscopes are electronically controlled and provide bi-ocular observation, range estimation, and are fitted for photography. An advanced ESM system uses the periscope antenna and there is also a special ESM antenna on its own mast. The ESM system provides multi-target detection and analysis, with high bearing accuracy. Radar provides target range and bearing at periscope depth and general navigational assistance.

The Action Information Organisation/Fire-Control system has a multiple display with a high computer capacity — matched to sensor capability. Two computers are provided, either of which is capable of driving the maximum data handling load. There are three display consoles but the system can operate on one. A large-scale tactical auto-plot is also provided.

A digital data bus is fitted to cater for

From the maxims of Max

● by Vice-Admiral Max K Horton, DSO, Flag Officer Submarines, addressing hard-pressed submarine crews at Malta in September, 1941

It is essential to keep the standard high — nothing can be neglected. It is not a kindness to overlook slackness or mistakes, it is really great cruelty to do so — cruelty to wives and relatives of the man you let off, and his shipmates and to yourself. There is no margin for mistakes in submarines, you are either alive or dead.

Max Horton, 1883-1951, first commanded a submarine aged 22. Apart from a two-year break he remained in submarines for the next 15 years. In the first world war he was the first submariner to sink an enemy warship, Hela. The Germans referred to the Baltic as Horton's sea. In the second world war he became Vice-Admiral Submarines and then Commander-in-Chief Western Approaches. He personally accepted the surrender of German U-boats at Londonderry

the complex flow of data between sensors, the AI0 and the fore-ends. A dual redundant bus provides high integrity in the data transmission system with a minimum of wiring between equipments. A semi-automatic plotting table, linked to the data bus, has its own built-in processor. Other navigational aids include Omega and Decca systems, compasses and an electromagnetic log.

Summary

Diesel-electric submarines — 'conventional' submarines — will continue to serve important roles in maritime operations. Costs apart, there are certain circumstances where not even the nuclear submarine can be as effective. Countries with long coastlines to defend or requiring ocean-going capability need a new class of conventional large submarine for which the Type 2400 has been developed. It represents an extension of technology derived from Vickers nuclear programme for the Royal Navy, combined with expertise gained from the building of more than 300 submarines over 80 years for home and overseas naval customers. Long-lead orders have already been placed for the boat and the order for the first-of-class for the RN is expected to be placed before the end of 1983. Designed in close association with the navy, the Type 2400 will have a submerged displacement of 2400 tonnes to accept a wide variety of weapon fits, fire-control systems and communications equipment.

The design sets new standards in habitability, reliability and operational availability and is expected to provide an exceptional patrol submarine facility into the 21st century.

Perisher – the path to submarine command

THE IMPORTANCE of the right man in command was recognised from the earliest days of the submarine service. One of the first Inspecting Captains of Submarines, Captain Roger Keyes, wrote, *'The military value of a submarine lies in the skill of her captain and in his powers of leadership. If you can add the "hunter's" instinct to a first-class eye and steady nerve, you will probably have a first-class submarine captain. But skill in attack is not enough. Unless the captain has the absolute confidence of his crew, unless the crew is trained to the highest pitch, and unless the machinery and weapons are maintained in the highest state of efficiency, you will not have a first-class submarine.'*

In 1919, Rear Admiral (Submarines) commissioned a study to ensure that the lessons of the war should not be forgotten. Included was an investigation into the qualities considered necessary to become a submarine captain, coolness, thoroughness, patience, keenness and the ability to make rapid decisions. In the use of the periscope for attacking, the fundamental skill was an ability to range accurately and to 'inclinate' on a target by merely looking at it. Other recommendations included the

● by Captain John Lang, RN who commanded HMS Walrus (SSK) 1972-1973, HMS Renown (SSBN) — Port crew — 1976-1978 and the Commanding Officer's Qualifying Course (the 'Perisher') 1979-1980. He is now in command of HMS Beaver, a new type 22 frigate

Above, Lieutenant Commander Andy Johnson, a successful Perisher subsequently appointed to command HMS Onyx, carrying out an attack, and pictured left, Teacher, Commander John Lang (left), 'washes up' an attack in the wardroom of HMS Onyx

importance of studying international law and blockade. Embryo captains were enjoined to look after their eyesight and it was noticed that officers who excelled at games of skill made good captains, whereas the nervous did not.

A formal commanding officers' training course, later to be known as the Commanding Officers Qualifying Course, evolved. Its predecessor had been called the Periscope School whence the COQC derived its somewhat ominous nickname, the 'Perisher', with the students being known as the perishers. From its inception, the purpose of the Perisher was to train commanding officers to attack. Initial training was carried out in the Attack Teacher at *HMS Dolphin*, Gosport. In an underground full scale model of a submarine's control room the

student would look through a periscope to see a surround of canvas realistically painted to represent sky, horizon and sea. Moving on a clockwork trolley came his target alone or escorted doing any speed and zig-zag pre-set by the course instructor. Such training helped develop the students' sense of location and a clear mental picture of his position relative to his target.

The Second World War saw a massive expansion in submarine building with a consequent increase in the number of students on the COQC which might include RN, RNR and RNVR officers from the Dutch, Polish, Greek or Norwegian navies. After a period in the attack teacher more realistic training at sea in a submarine followed. Successful students emerged as qualified commanding officers capable of taking a submarine into action in any circumstances.

At the war's end, a peacetime pattern emerged with three to four courses being held annually with up to six students on each, some entirely foreign students; their reputation for excellence already established. By the 1960s the Dutch, Australians and Canadians were regular attenders while Denmark, Portugal, Norway, Israel and Germany sent occasional representatives. The non-English pass rate was impressively high.

The 1960s, however, were a time for change. Nuclear power had arrived and the wire-guided torpedo was beginning to replace the faithful 30-year-old Mk VIII salvo torpedo. Submarines were larger, faster and equipped with more effective sensors but the aspiring captain was still required to develop split second timing qualities, an ice cool nerve and the ability to make accurate decisions under stress. An increasing proportion of the training was carried out at sea.

By the 1970s the course had evolved further. Sea training included more advanced attacking techniques, particularly against other submarines. Operations were conducted in areas monitored by 'hostile' aircraft and little sympathy was given to the CO who allowed himself to be detected by patrolling Nimrod or Sea King. Surveillance techniques were introduced and, most demanding of all, special operations were conducted involving the landing and recovery of Royal Marine Special Boat Section units on an unfriendly shore at night. Such activities were not for the faint-hearted. Over the years the failure rate remained consistent at 30%.

Today, two COQC courses are run annually each with 12 students, including foreigners, divided into two groups, and each with its own teacher. After an introduction of some two to three weeks when the perishers are lectured on matters as diverse as the nature of today's maritime threat, oceanography, and the effects of fatigue on decision making, the course gets down to attack. Starting in the modern equivalent of the Attack Teacher, now computerised and more akin to a real submarine, the students relearn old principles. The ability to operate safely in the close vicinity of fast surface ships is as relevant today as it ever was despite

the introduction of new long-range weapons. Two to three weeks of intensive sea training follows with the perishers embarking each day in a conventional submarine to operate from dawn to dusk against modern frigates and destroyers. During this time the teacher is usually able to identify those unable to cope with the various pressures and, towards the end of this phase, will inform the unsuccessful candidates, over a tot of whisky, that they are being withdrawn from further training.

This attacking phase could be described as an aptitude test whereas once its successful completion was

Tracks of a Perisher's torpedoes speeding on their way to the target. For these exercises the weapons are set to run deep. It is obvious why modern electric weapons, which leave no visible track, are advantageous but they are not as fast as the old Mk 8** torpedoes

Officers of COQC No 35 in 1933 standing by the torpedo collision heads which prove that their final Perisher attacks had been sucessful. Collision heads have not been fitted to torpedoes for many years but they left no room for doubt about whether or not a hit had been scored!

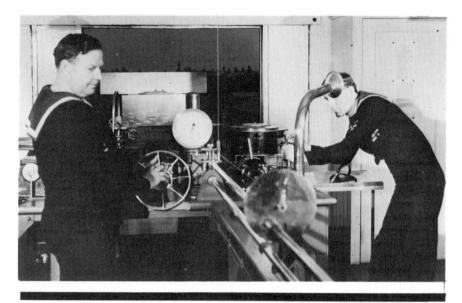

The rudimentary old type of shore attack teacher in use during World War II. Although this was adequate for its time much more sophisticated simulators are required today.
Syndicated Features Ltd

tantamount to qualifying. No longer. A more complex and demanding second phase follows. The perishers spend more time in the Command Team Trainers before a further few weeks sea time in an exercise code-named Cockfight. Each perisher takes it in turn to be the CO, tackling any problem presented. The incidents are designed to stretch the individual and to provide experience. Awkward defects may arise, sailors develop unpleasant illnesses (the quality of some acting deserves acclaim from the most critical theatre-goers), and conflicting priorities will tax his captaincy. Night attacks are introduced, hostile aircraft appear at the most inconvenient moments and fishing boats appear from nowhere to lay nets 1,000 yards in front of an advancing submarine. The students never cease to wonder how teacher dreams them up.

On one Cockfight, a perisher was conducting some particularly complex operation when a chef, covered in blood and in an advanced state of shock, staggered into the control room having just 'chopped' off one of his fingers. The finger fell at the foot of the startled captain who, wondering what to do next, was horrified to see the second panel watchkeeper pick up the 'finger' and eat it knowing it to be only a chipolata. The captain, who didn't, nearly fainted.

During Cockfight the CO faces increasingly complex problems but as sea time progresses, his confidence grows and with it his ability to handle the unexpected. He will frighten himself at least once but, with the ever watchful eye of teacher behind him, will learn to press himself to the limit. As Captain Keyes said 70 years ago the military value of a submarine lies in the skill of her captain which is as true today as then.

And it's the Perisher that sees to it.

The cardinal crime is to be put deep by Teacher to avoid collision. This periscope photograph of HMS Ambuscade suggests that Teacher is about to order the submarine to safe depth if the Perisher does not do so immediately. The rule is that the boat must go deep if an approaching ship is within one minute's run at its maximum speed plus an assumed submarine speed of eight knots: in practice nowadays this means going deep when the range is about 1,300 yards

Netherlands submarines

TWELVE HUNDRED reunionists stood with their heads bowed when their Queen, Queen Beatrix, laid a wreath at the memoral to the Dutch submariners who gave their lives during the second world war. The day was May 28, 1982, the occasion the celebration of the 75th anniversary of the Royal Netherlands Navy submarine service. The ex-submariners had come from all over the world to participate in the celebration; the oldest, a 94-year-old Stoker Petty Officer, had been a member of the first Dutch submarine commissioned on December 20 1906.

Indeed, it all started in 1906 when the Flushing Dockyard Company 'De Schelde' built a submarine on its own account, following the design of John Philip Holland. Examples of this type of boat were already in service with the British and US navies. When proved a success, it was bought by the navy and commissioned as the *O1* (O for Onderzeeboot). Submarine building continued in the Netherlands using increasingly original designs. By 1913 the navy had five boats. In that same year the first boat was launched specifically designed for service in the Netherlands East Indies (now Indonesia). The first two of this type were towed to the Far East, but the third one, *KIII*, in 1920 made the long voyage under her own power. These submarines were the first ever to operate in the Far East.

By 1934 the Dutch submarine service consisted of more than 30 boats, serving in Europe and in the Indies. Several of the boats became well known as a result of their voyages with Professor Vening Meinesz who wanted to measure the earth's gravity in several places to determine the movement of the continents. Thus *K12*, *K13* and *K18* made voyages either through the Panama Canal to the East Indies, or via

● by Captain J Kleijn, Royal Netherlands Navy, who joined submarines in 1958, did his Perisher command course with the British Royal Navy in 1967 and commanded the submarines Zeehond and Dolfyn in 1978. He has been head of the Netherlands Submarine Squadron since 1980

Captain Jack Kleijn RNLN, head of the Netherlands submarine service

South America, the Cape of Good Hope and Australia to Java and the Indonesian archipelago. Apart from the interesting scientific findings the voyages produced much submarine experience from which later boats benefited greatly.

In 1934 plans were made for a series of nine more submarines. The aftermath of the world crisis and consequent low budgets caused delays but in 1936 the keel was laid for *O19*. This series had an ingenious device by which the submarine could run its diesel engines while submerged. It consisted of two tubes which extended above the water level when the boat was at periscope depth — one for fresh air to enter the boat and the other as an exhaust. This system later became known world-wide as the 'schnorchel' or 'snort'. When the Germans invaded the Netherlands in 1940 they discovered the device on board boats under construction in the Dutch yards. They removed it as being too dangerous but, later on, installed it on all their U-boats.

During the second world war Dutch submarines joined the Allies in European and Mediterranean waters as well as in the Far East. Seven boats were lost and several others, mainly the older boats, were scrapped or used as targets for anti-submarine training. When the

Like many other navies the Dutch fleet adopted J P Holland's design for its first submarine 01. The boat was commissioned in 1906 and served until 1920. Shown far right is HNLMS Zwaardvis, commissioned in 1972, has a top speed of 20 knots submerged and is an excellent general-purpose patrol submarine. The equipment, capabilities and training of Netherlands submarines have always been first-class and they are much respected by other navies

war ended six boats were left: three of the O type, two of the famous British T-class which were built for the Netherlands Government and one T-class on loan from the Royal Navy. Later, in 1953, two American 'Guppy' fleet submarines were borrowed from the USA to replace the oldest boats. The number of submarines has remained at six since that time. With that number co-operation began with the other nations in the newly formed NATO alliance.

New construction

Continuing the old tradition and using the experience gained during the war, the Dutch planned the construction of new submarines. During the war most boats had a maximum diving depth of 100 to 120 metres (300 - 400 feet); but in light of new sonar equipment and weapons a depth of 200 metres seemed necessary. The quality of the available steel and the welding techniques at the time were not good enough to construct a boat with one hull of, say, 1,800 tons to reach that depth. It was decided therefore to construct three smaller hulls and combine them in one submarine, thus permitting a lighter construction while retaining the ability

to withstand the requisite increased pressure. In 1954 the keels of two submarines of this unique design, the 'triple hull' type, were laid at the Rotterdam Drydock Company. Delays during building, mainly as a result of cuts in the navy's budget, delayed the launching of the first boat *Dolfijn* until 1959 and *Zeehond* until 1960. Around that time improved construction techniques made it possible to construct a single hulled boat that could dive to 200 metres and more. As the design proved to be a good one, two more boats, *Potvis* and *Tonijn* were commissioned in 1965.

Proof that the Netherlands submarines were ready for their task came in 1962 when Indonesia laid claim to that part of the island of New Guinea still governed by the Dutch. As war threatened, the Dutch Government enlarged its fighting forces on and around that island. Among them were *Dolfijn* and the Guppy *Zeeleeuw*, both of which made the long voyage from Europe via the Panama canal and the Pacific Ocean, to be followed by the Guppy *Walrus*. Although several patrols were made, no boat saw action. *Zeeleeuw* and *Dolfijn* circumnavigated the world by returning to the Netherlands via the Cape of Good Hope and the Suez canal

respectively, while *Walrus* returned home precisely the way she had come.

At the beginning of the 60s a staff requirement was raised for another class of submarines. The conventional outer appearance of submarines was abandoned and, following the lines of the *USS Albacore* and *USS Barbel*, a teardrop hull-shape was adopted, a design that could have contained nuclear propulsion. But the costs for research and building of such a plant and its subsequent maintenance were, relatively, so high for a small navy such as the Dutch that the idea for a nuclear propulsion plant had to be abandoned. The new boats, *Zwaardvis* and *Tijgerhaai*, were equipped therefore with conventional diesel-electric propulsion; they were launched in 1970 and 1971 respectively.

Taking a closer look at these boats, we notice first the hull-shape, like a whale, without the old-fashioned superstructure but with everything as streamlined as possible apart from the inevitable fin standing out as an outer protection for the periscopes, ECM masts, radio mast and snort mast. The forward diving planes protrude like wings of an aircraft. Placing the forward diving planes in the bow would have interfered with the main sonar and its

construction in the bulbous nose, together with the siting of the torpedo tubes, would have been too complicated. As usual in modern submarines the boats have only one propeller, which makes manoeuvering in harbour and on the surface more difficult. But of course these boats were designed to operate *under* water; their performance on the surface is not critical. Inside the bow are the six torpedo tubes and a spacious torpedo room. The tubes can launch a variety of torpedoes to the maximum diving depth of the boat and 14 reload torpedoes can be carried in the torpedo room. Torpedo handling and loading is done hydraulically. The torpedo room is not meant to serve as an accommodation space as well; so the old custom of lodging the crew together with the torpedoes does not apply on board *Zwaardvis*-class boats.

A single escape tower is mounted in the deckhead of the torpedo room. This escape tower is a small watertight cylinder with room for one man so that, after an accident, the crew can leave the boat individually. Once a man is inside, the lower lid is shut and the small compartment filled with water. After equalising with the external pressure the upper lid is opened and the man floats to the surface. The escape tower can also be used for attack swimmers who can leave the boat while submerged and re-enter after their job is done.

The centre section of the boat contains, on three decks, the main batteries, the crew accommodation space, the galley and mess and, on the top deck, the officers' accommodation, radio room, sound room and control room.

The batteries consist of more than 400 battery cells, each about three feet high and weighing 500 kgs to propel the boat submerged. Underwater speeds are higher than surface, due to the shape of the boat, and easily reach the 20 knot mark.

Accommodation on the middle deck is roomy by submarine standards, each rating having his own bunk with a reading light and locker for his belongings. In total the crew of a *Zwaarduis* class submarine consists of nine officers, 15 chief petty officers and 43 petty officers and junior ratings. Standards required of the crew are high; apart from physical fitness and a good theoretical training they must be able to endure long and often monotonous patrols. In the Dutch navy it takes a rating, after his medical examination and initial training, more than a year to qualify for submarine service. If at the

HNLMS Dolfyn, one of four triple-hulled submarines with a diving depth of 980 ft (300m). With a maximum submerged speed of 17 knots and eight torpedo tubes (4 bow, 4 stern) this class, although now about 20 years old, is still powerful

end of the year he passes he is given his 'dolphins' as a sign of his membership of an exclusive group. The age limit for service in Dutch conventional submarines is 35 years for officers and 40 years for chief petty officers.

The CPO's are accommodated in a separate mess sharing three cabins. The centre part of the middle deck, the junior rates' mess, is where meals are eaten and movies shown — the focal point of social life. Around it are the galley, the provisions locker, the deep freeze and refrigerator for the stowage and preparation of food. When, after six hours on duty (Dutch routine is six hours on, six hours off), the smell of cooking pervades the submarine a man must not be disappointed in the quality or quantity of the meals. The cook's contribution to morale is vital.

Two- or three-berth cabins for officers are on the top deck where the equipment necessary to navigate and fight the boat is also placed, the radio and radar equipment, the electronic support measures (ESM) and a sound room in which the sonar, the underwater listening gear, is housed. In the control room itself the centre piece is formed by two periscopes — an attack periscope with a slender head and a navigation periscope which is bifocal

and has, consequently, a broader head. The former, smaller instrument is used at close quarters against surface ships to reduce the possibility of being spotted visually or by radar. On the port side is a panel with course and depth controls which look something like the control column in an aircraft. Both forward and after hydroplanes can be operated separately but they can also be combined into a one-man control position.

The fire-control equipment, plotting table and navigational aids are mounted to starboard. Due to the longer reach of modern wire-guided torpedoes and the increasingly refined detection systems, attacks made by submarines are mostly carried out at depth and can last for several hours. Such an action can start, however, within minutes. This puts a great strain on the crew who, while waiting patiently, must be ready to come into action in a matter of minutes and then maintain their concentration for several hours during an attack. Officers are trained in Holland, but must join the British Commanding Officers Qualifying Course (COQC) before appointment as captain of a submarine.

From the ratings' mess one enters, via a small door, the third part of the boat — the engine room and electrical

manoeuvring position. In the engine room three diesel generators dominate the scene. Together with their auxiliary equipment they form, to the outsider, an incredible maze of pipes and apparatus. Abaft the engine room the electrical switchboard looks like the cockpit of a modern aircraft with all its meters, knobs and handled. Power from the batteries or diesel generators is distributed here, either to the main electric motor which drives the propeller shaft or to recharge the battery after a period of submerged operations.

Dutch submarines, although limited in number, are among the most advanced conventional boats the western world can provide and they form, together with the submarines of the other NATO countries, a formidable weapon for safeguarding the western world.

Two new boats are under construction in Rotterdam currently, their outer shape differing little from the *Zwaardvis* class boats. But the crew has been reduced considerably from 67 men to 50 men for far greater automation and computerisation has taken place. Modern weapons will be installed and the propulsion plant gives the submarines both a higher speed and one which can be maintained for a long time.

Bootle's bucket

● by Richard Compton-Hall

SOME PEOPLE CELEBRATE the New Year with a resolution — or even two. Others do it with a glass — or even three. But submariners — let's face it — are different. Flag Officer Submarines decided that the First of January was a splendid time to inspect something. 'And,' as he jovially asked his Staff, 'what better than a submarine? Just the way to start the New Year off all bright-eyed and bushy-tailed.'

The Flotilla Engineer Officer moaned quietly. He allowed a furry, blackened tongue to protrude slightly between dried lips.

'Let's start with the oldest boat in the Service,' FOSM went on, politely ignoring the reactions of his Staff.

The oldest boat in the service received the news without noticeable enthusiasm. In several ways it was not the ideal choice. The Captain suffered severely from promotionitis; the Navigator always went to pieces at inspections and got lost; and then . . . and then there was Bootle, Leading Stoker Bootle.

The First Lieutenant of Bootle's submarine was tall, cultured and distinguished. Bootle was not. The elegant Number One and the small, wizened, oily Chief Stoker's Mate were incompatible — as the Captain, who had marital problems, often pointed out.

When Number One joined the submarine, Bootle had already established himself as a cave-dweller, working (between naps and frequent pauses for refreshment) mainly in thè bilges. It was on return from one of his visits to the nether regions that Bootle initially came to the First Lieutenant's shuddering notice. Number One was contentedly admiring the newly-painted white surround of the hatch leading down to the Auxiliary Machinery Space when, without warning, a gnarled and oily disembodied hand appeared from below. For a moment the paw waved blindly before fastening on the coaming. Little rivulets of oil ran slowly down the fresh paint. Next came a bucket — a bent and battered bucket filled to the brim with mercifully indescribable objects floating in a greasy, bilgey soup. The bucket wavered uncertainly above the hatchway before descending heavily onto the sparkling Control Room deck, its hideous contents slopping over onto the polished tiles.

When, at last, some jagged spikes of hair appeared, followed by Bootle's wrinkled, oil-streaked features, Number One could only ask, faintly, where the apparition had come from. 'Bin down Snort Drain Two,' grunted Bootle.

From that time, Bootle was widely referred to throughout the submarine service as 'the Thing from snort drain two'.

Bootle's bucket was permanently attached to him. He carried it everywhere and he left it parked outside his mess at night.

An inspection brings all normal work to a halt. Anything untidy must temporarily be lodged in the next-door submarine or otherwise hidden. It was quite unthinkable that either Bootle or the bucket should be visible to the Admiral.

The Admiral was scheduled to 'walk through' the submarine — a lesser deal than a full inspection. 'Walking through' is an expression denoting that the walker tacitly agrees not to look in holes and corners where he might find something embarrassing or disagreeable. Bootle could safely be left on board for this part of the ceremonies; the Admiral had to take his chance of coming up against him. But for Divisions, when the

'What', he asked gently, 'is that?'

entire Ship's Company were to line up on the jetty — definitely *no*. The Admiral could not be allowed to take the risk of a formal bodily encounter.

During Divisions, said the First Lieutenant, Bootle could remain on board the submarine and clean out the engine-room bilges. When not otherwise occupied he was not to stray outside the stokers' mess. Apart from a general appearance of it being New Year's Day following New Year's Eve, the inspection went much as such inspections tend to go.

The Flotilla Engineer Officer poked the pressure hull with the butt-end of a wheel-spanner. No water came in, even at a second attempt, and FEO mentally registered the boat as good for another couple of commissions. He paused as he passed Bootle's mess.

'Any trouble with old age?' he asked.

Bootle knew FEO would like an honest answer, him being an Engineer. 'Well, when I goes ashore, like, it's not the same . . . I seen the doctor mind . . .'

The Captain, the First Lieutenant, the Chief Stoker and the Navigator had by now congregated in the doorway. It sounded like one voice, 'BOOTLE!'

The plan for the Admiral to walk quickly through the submarine and then inspect Divisions worked quite well. Bootle, safe and sound in the comforting dimness of the bilges, had not been seen since the Admiral came on board. The Captain marched onto the jetty with a confident tread while the Admiral retired to allow time for the Ship's Company to fall in for Divisions which Bootle had entirely forgotten about, for tot-time was coming up. Grasping his beloved bucket he prepared to emerge.

Flag Officer Submarines returned for Divisions after a quick gin in his office. A scratch band from the barracks had a go at *the Garb of Old Gaul;* the Coxswain coaxed the Ship's Company to attention; the Captain offered his hand absent-mindedly; and the Navigator genuflected. Everyone did his best to make the occasion memorable.

The Admiral complimented the crew on their smartness.
'Is this the lot?'
'Yessir,' lied the Captain.
'No black sheep, eh?' laughed the Admiral.

Then it happened. Blood drained from the First Lieutenant's face. He had the feeling that this was where he had come in. An oily paw appeared through the open engine-room hatch and waved itself around — apparently in friendly greeting to the Admiral. It was followed by a battered, shapeless metal object which was lowered tenderly onto the casing. The Navigator recovered first. 'Down Bootle,' he shouted, 'down.' He had dogs at home.

Flag Officer Submarines had earned his rank for cool command.
'What,' he asked gently, 'is that?'
The Captain tried hard.
'It's a b-bucket, sir. B-Bootle's bucket.'

Flag Officer Submarines nodded, with understanding, and walked with head bowed to the official car. For he too had been a submarine captain himself once. He knew that there were intimate family matters in the domestic life of a submarine that even a Flag Officer should not question.
'Happy New Year,' he murmured sympathetically, 'and the best of British luck to you — and Bootle.'

New U-Boats

● by Kapitän Zur See Hannes Ewerth (Commander of the Submarine Flotilla of the Federal German Navy) pictured below

THE ORIGINS of the German term 'Uboot' (U-Boat), short for 'Unterseeboot' (literally undersea boat) go back to the turn of the century when the first 'undersea warships' — a name given by Wilhelm Bauer to a boat constructed by him in 1850 — were introduced in the German Fleet. Although earlier inventions, like Fulton's *Nautilus* and Bushnell's *Turtle,* had been designed similarly, classifying these submersibles as 'undersea vessels' would have been premature.

Even in Germany the use of submarines was controversial until the beginning of World War I, but Grand Admiral von Tirpitz had already recognized their potential and had encouraged their development and construction. Before the submarine was accepted in the Imperial Navy certain reservations had to be overcome. Most naval officers then associated the submarine with something dishonourable, because its submersibility enabled it to fight unseen.

The breakthrough came with Otto Weddigen who, in *U9,* succeeded in sinking the British cruisers *Hogue, Cressy* and *Aboukir* one morning during World War I and proved the submarine's potential. (See *Three Before Breakfast* by Alan Coles, Mason, £6.95). From 1906 until 1918 a total of 374 U-boats were built for the Imperial Navy and sank

6,394 ships during World War I.

The year 1918 marked the end of the first era of German submarines. In the early years of the Reichsmarine no U-boats were designed or built. It was not until the commissioning of *U1* in June 1935 that the foundation was laid for the world's largest submarine fleet. The successes of 1,171 U-boats had a decisive impact on the conduct of naval warfare from 1939 to 1945 until the end of the war seemingly sealed the fate of German submarines for ever. But the unexpected was still to happen.

In the Paris Agreements of October 23, 1954, the level of German military forces was set. However, in the 'Accord Special' the Federal Republic of Germany was allowed to build small submarines of not more than 350 tons because of its strategic geographical position at the Baltic approaches.

Developments and reorganization

The mission of the Navy *to protect the territory of the litoral NATO member states and the Baltic Approaches by warding off attacks against the coast of the North Sea and the Baltic; to impede, on a temporary and local basis, enemy operations in the Baltic; to deny the enemy the use of the lines of communication between the Baltic and the North Sea; and to enable the use of the North Sea in the interest of the Alliance* formed the basis for the construction of 12 submarines, approved by the Bundestag in 1956.

First, priority had to be given to training crews. Two World War II Type XXIII submarines were lifted, repaired and commissioned in August and October 1957 under the name of *U Hai* and *U Hecht* respectively. On September 1, 1960, *U Wilhelm Bauer*, a former Type XXI submarine followed. These early submarines were placed under the command of the Amphibious Forces and assigned to a reactivated Submarine Training Group at Neustadt where training was resumed after a break of 12 years.

So 25 years ago the organization of a German submarine force began for the third time. In 1958 Class 201 submarines designed by the Ingenieurkontor Lübeck were selected and construction started at the Howaldtswerke Deutsche Werft AG shipyards. On March 20, 1962, the first submarine of the Federal German Navy, *U1*, was commissioned and assigned to the 1st Submarine Squadron at Kiel. In the same year *U2* was also commissioned, while *U3*, designated *U Kobben*, sailed under the Norwegian flag and later redeployed to Neustadt to serve as a training vessel. Despite the promising beginning, setbacks soon followed. The anti-magnetic steel developed signs of intergranular stress corrosion, so that *U1* and *U2* had to be refitted with new pressure hulls, now made of ferritic steel (due to financial stringency).

The second series of submarines, *U4* to *U8*, enlarged to 450 tons due to relaxed WEU regulations and designated Class 205, proved to be more sea-water resistant. However, still another

Crew of U29 before sailing. The complement of a Type 206 total only four officers and 18 men

SUBMARINE FLOTILLA KIEL				
1st SUBMARINE SQUADRON KIEL		**3rd SUBMARINE SQUADRON ECKERNFÖRDE**		**SUBMARINE TRAINING GROUP NEUSTADT**
U1	U25	U13	U19	**FIRST COMPANY** **INDIVIDUAL TRAINING**
U2	U26	U14	U20	
U9	U27	U15	U21	**SECOND COMPANY** **SUBMARINE ESCAPE TRAINING**
U10	U28	U16	U22	
U11	U29	U17	U23	
U12	U30	U18	U24	
TENDER LAHN		**TENDER LECH**		

The depot ship Lahn supporting the First Submarine Squadron. The small size and considerable discomfort of modern U-boats make depot ships a necessity besides allowing a high degree of operational flexibility

construction programme was needed before *U9* to *U12,* now definitely corrosion-proof, could be commissioned between 1967 and 1969. It was not until this latter date that the 1st Submarine Squadron was provided with six fully operational submarines.

With the adoption of the NATO strategy of Flexible Response the Navy's concept was modified: *to counter a possible threat as far seawards as possible; to impede enemy operations in the Baltic and to contain enemy forces; and to use the North Sea for the movement of supplies.*

Following Bundestag approval to raise the strength of the submarine force to 30, the development of 24 class 206 submarines principally designed for the Baltic and of six submarines each with a displacement of 1,000 for the North Sea began. The latter were to be employed in an SSK-role (submarine-submarine-killer). This series, later reduced to 18 Class 206 submarines due to lack of funds, was constructed at the Howaldtswerke Deutsche Werft AG and Thyssen Nordseewerft shipyards until 1975 and subsequently commissioned at bi-monthly intervals. Construction of the larger submarines was cancelled, again due to cash shortage.

Since May 1975 the Submarine Flotilla has had 24 submarines at its command. Its structure and organization is shown in the organizational chart. The delivery of the new submarines and the installation of the appropriate weapons completed the 'Weapons System Class 206 Submarines'. Now the main effort had to be directed towards crew training which was divided into two stages: that of individuals in accordance with their future shipboard functions assignments; and shipboard training of the crew as a homogeneous team. The old concept of theory in the classroom and learning-by-doing aboard was no longer satisfactory.

The usual naval specialist shipboard training had to be complemented by a basic training course for submariners carried out by the Submarine Training Group at Neustadt/Holstein, and encompassing both theoretical and practical shipboard instruction. Here emphasis was placed on individual shipboard specialty training, ie an engineman or a watch officer would receive his specialist training with theory and practice well-balanced.

When the submariner goes on board he is virtually fully qualified but the commander's close supervision is needed. It is the latter's task to see that integration is smooth, and that training is adapted to the specific conditions in his submarine. It is also his responsibility to meld his crew who must learn to operate the submarine submerged for several weeks, to maintain and, if necessary, to repair its systems and equipment with the sole objective of being ready for action when required.

After completion of intensive individual training in the Baltic, North Sea or the Skagerrak under the commander's direction the squadron commander will conduct a readiness-for-sea and readiness-for-submergence inspection. This demonstrates the crew's ability to handle and navigate the submarine safely during surfaced and submerged operations.

Following the individual training Submerged Operations Combat Training (TTG) is carried out and evaluated by the Training Group TTG. The crew must now be able to control the submarine under operational conditions surfaced or submerged. The time has still not come for the commander, who has the sole responsibility for the training of his crew, to report his submarine ready for action, because team training for ordnance delivery has still to be conducted.

Although every sensor or weapons system operator has received system-related training, ordnance training integrates the output from the different stations, ie the information gathered by individual operators, into an operational sequence so that the data needed for aimed torpedo firing can be processed.

A specially designed simulator (submarine system trainer) — a shore-based CIC — is used for this purpose. In this connection the saying dating back to the old days of the Navy,

You ask me, friend what theory is?
A thing that's supposed to work and never does.
And what is practice?
A thing that works and nobody knows why!

might be quoted with some justification in recognition of the achievements of wartime-submariers despite less elaborate training facilities. For current training of CIC-teams, however, this simulator-trainer system is essential.

After five months' training the operational programme ends with a torpedo 'wet shot' when commander and crew prove they are a well co-ordinated, efficient and reliable team, capable of locating, identifying/classifying and attacking the enemy from the depth of the sea.

Conclusion

The submarines are an integral part of the fleet, but when operating at sea

under Flag Officer, Germany, they are left to their own devices and operate at their own discretion. Thus the commander gives the order; the commander makes decisions; and the commander assumes responsibility! Whether during NATO or national exercises, with Flag Officer Sea Training (FOST) or at the Joint Maritime Course (JMC), these submarines have always furnished proof of their ability to cope with their assigned tasks.

Their mission has not changed during the last 25 years. But what has had a decisive impact on operational planning and tactics is the enormous expansion of the Soviet fleet and the development of sensors and weapons. Only a few features link our present-day submarines with U-boats of the past. Submerged operations sustained for weeks and the far longer range of weapons, as well as the ability to identify and attack targets from the depths of the sea without recourse to optical or optronic sensors, have transformed the submarine into an implement capable of operating effectively in all waters under the severest enemy threats.

On the left is shown U12, the last of 6 Type 205 boats, commissioned January 14, 1969, and right, Wilhelm Bauer, a type XXI (ex U-2540). Scuttled May 3, 1945, raised in 1957 and rebuilt, this boat served until 1982. The revolutionary Type XXI U-boats were, fortunately for the Allies, not in time to be operational during the war

Trials and tribulations in a T-boat

SOMETIMES, when taking more notice than usual of my thinning hair, I start reminiscing and the name of one Able Seaman Murray, or 'Young Murray' as we called him, comes to mind to take some responsibility for the grey locks.

It all began 40 years ago. Young Murray had been conscripted into the Navy and, after basic training followed by a course in radar, was sent via the Submarine Training School to his first sea-going vessel — A T class submarine of which I was then Coxswain. He was just a month or two past his 19th birthday, a little Scots laddie that you just had to like. He was just five feet one and a quarter in seaboots and weighed in at around seven stone.

Small though he was, Murray was a Mobile Nautical Disaster Area — the proverbial accident looking for somewhere to happen. It eventually reached the point when even the Captain, on occasion, would say, 'Cox'n, find out what Murray is up to — and *stop him*.'

Radar in those days was not the exact science it appears to be today and frequently, after a sharp-eyed lookout had been observing a ship for some considerable time, the radar operator's Scottish voice would issue forth from the bridge voicepipe and proudly explain that on a certain bearing there could be seen 'an object, sirr'.

Mint Murray

Perhaps Murray's not quite all-seeing eye got him off to an undeservedly poor start. But before long we realised that things happened sooner or later when Murray was around. We coped quite well with the Germans, the Italians and the Japanese who were more predictable in their habits. But with Young Murray — well, perhaps a few examples will help to explain the problem.

Once, we were patrolling off Toulon when he took over the helm for a spell. I had been listening purposely while the necessary information was turned over to him by the man he was relieving and I noticed a puzzled look on Young Murray's face. Here I should explain that the compass repeater the helmsman had to watch continually, and which indicated our course, was the usual endless tape marked in degrees — 0 representing north, 090 east, 180

● by George Luck DSM, the youngest seaman CPO ever in the Royal Navy — one month before his 21st birthday; and the youngest submarine Coxswain when he assumed his duties in HMS Taurus at Algiers in February, 1943. He rose from Boy 1st Class to Chief Petty Officer in a little less than three years. However, RN Coxswains are rightly given a standing far beyond their years. In fact the men who fought the underwater war in British submarines and German U-boats were mostly very young and, exceptionally, the Captain might be only 21 years old himself. The hero of George Luck's story was only a couple of years his junior; but it would have been entirely natural to call him 'Young Murray'

HMS Taurus with the Coxswain (and author of this story) on the gun platform at right. The Jolly Roger shows clearly how successful the boat was under Lieutenant M R V Wingfield (bridge at centre): the bars indicate successful torpedo attacks on surface ships and one U-boat; the stars indicate gun-actions; the figure at the top shows that 24 mines were laid; and the daggers stand for clandestine 'cloak-and-dagger' operations

south, 270 west, and back to 0.

Young Murray duly took over and the routine settled down. A little while later, the officer of the watch, a young sub-lieutenant (who was later to be knighted and become the Second Sea Lord) asked in a quiet but distinctly ominous voice if I would find out what on earth Young Murray was supposed to be doing. Going over to the wheel, I saw the young stalwart sitting back in his seat reading a book and happily humming to himself. Gently (as submarine Cox'ns are wont to do in such circumstances) I politely suggested that he might care to attend to his steering.

Looking hurt, Young Murray asked, 'what are we stopped for 'Swain?' Furiously, I pointed to the telegraph repeaters and the revolution counter which showed half ahead and a healthy 300 revolutions respectively. His reply was to indicate the zero on the gyro repeater and say, 'if we're nay stopped, why are no goin' anywhere the noo?'

We just happened to be steering due north! (Murray came off the wheel).

A flash and a bang

There was another jolly little happening soon afterwards. When the Captain deemed it safe to do so, to save precious time in harbour, we would top up the batteries with distilled water while returning submerged from patrol. This entailed lifting the deckplates covering the batteries, an operation carried out by the Petty Officer LTO and his electrical team. In the past I had sent Young Murray to assist various heads of departments if they had a spot of work to do like this. The usual response was a jocular, 'thanks a lot, what have you got against me?'

This time it was the turn of the POLTO to be 'assisted'. Young Murray had been given a dustpan and brush to clean the airtight seals around the deckplates. Surely, we thought, he was capable of doing that quite safely. Unfortunately, we overlooked the fact that in those days dustpans were made of metal so when our young friend nonchalantly placed his dustpan across the terminals of a battery cell it produced a flash, a bang, and a cloud of smoke and fumes which scared the wits out of everybody. Young Murray looked at the mangled remains and complained bitterly that no-one had told him 'yon battery was switched on'.

Fortunately nobody was hurt but it was a close shave.

Then came the frolic in Trincomalee harbour. A strong wind was making it difficult for us to secure to a buoy prior to swinging compasses. It was customary, when carrying out this normally simple little evolution, for a man to mount the buoy to secure either the cable or a heavy wire, an evolution known as 'jumping the buoy'. After a couple of futile attempts, frustrated by the wind, the Captain at last succeeded in manoeuvring the boat somewhere near striking distance. It was now or never. Glaring at me he ordered, 'get down there and get someone on that buoy immediately'.

I hurried to the fore-casing, saw Young Murray standing spare and ordered, 'jump the buoy. Do you know what you have to do?' something told me I had not made a wise choice when he replied all too confidently, 'och, that's nae problem at all'.

Scarcely reassured I sped back to the bridge. Young Murray thought a bit, turned to the bridge and shouted, 'Right then, let's be havin' ye.'

The Captain's next remark was, 'all right Cox'n. You put him there, let's find out what he wants.'

And so with shouts of 'up a bit . . . back a bit . . .', enough arm waving for a battleship's farewell and a final 'whoa . . . hold her there!' from the prospective buoy-jumper, we got within about 15 feet of the buoy. Motioning everyone to one side and fully in command of the situation, Young Murray secured one end of the heaving line around his midriff, the other end to our capstan and faced forward. From a standing start he hurtled along the casing and, like a Grand National winner at Aintree, literally took off, clearing the buoy with feet to spare. Spluttering, he surfaced and somehow managed to clamber onto the buoy, untie the flimsy heaving line from around his waist and secure it to the huge steel ring. Well satisfied he then faced the bridge smartly and called out triumphantly, as the line tautened and threatened to part, 'all secured up forrard the noo, sir. Ye can relax.'

Gravely the Captain turned to me, 'thank you very much, Cox'n. We must do that again sometime. Captain 'S' must be very impressed.' As all the foregoing had been witnessed by an interested depot ship and three or four other submarines, I don't think he meant it.

But my fondest memory is of Murray's amorous interlude at Colombo. To appreciate this you must visualise a tropical beach, palm trees, the whisper of the surf on silver sand, a big yellow moon — a typical Hollywood movie scene. With some messmates I was relaxing on the beach with a few bottles of canteen beer. The atmosphere was tranquil and peaceful. I think it was the Stoker PO who spoke first, 'blimey, take a look at this.'

'This' was Young Murray. He was rigged out in Empire Builder's shorts, pusser's boots, long black stockings (around his ankles), a white jumper (at least ten sizes too large) and, of all things, the biggest pith helmet imaginable. The sight of his diminutive figure inside this lot was arresting to say the least. However, Murray's companion was even more startling. She was a veritable amazon of a woman — all of six feet with long blonde hair and a 44-24-36 figure. She was wearing, barely, a bikini which would have failed the Trades Description Act if it had been in force in those days. She sinuated over towards us while Young Murray stomped alongside her through the soft sand. As the strangely assorted pair passed our group the face beneath the pith helmet grinned and chuckled something about, 'all right the noo.' His companion haughtily peered down at us over the starboard half of her 44, tossed her long tresses and glided on.

Squeaks and giggles

A little further along the beach they selected a spot for themselves and Young Murray dutifully scooped out a hollow into which they both snuggled. Soon there came little squeaks, giggles and other rapturous sounds. To say that we were dumbstruck is an understatement. And then it happened: *Swipe!* We all winced in sympathy and watched as the voluptuous amazon leapt to her feet. Everything trembled as she brushed off the sand and steamed off down the beach like the *Ark Royal* which also overhung at both ends.

Eventually Young Murray came over looking quite shattered. I naturally asked what had upset the fair damsel and, visibly affected, he said, 'och, 'Swain, there's no pleasin' yon big lassie. I've taken her for a taxi ride, we've had big eats, I've bought her sun glasses and lots more besides, then she said, "let's go down to the beach". I didna mind that. And then she started kissin' and cuddlin' and that was OK. Then, all of a rush, she said, "take me, take me". So ah said, "where the hell d'ye want tay go the noo, the pictures?" And then she belted me one.'

About three weeks later we were sitting on the bottom of the Malacca Strait off Penang, being depth-charged unmercifully, when Young Murray crawled over alongside me, forced a grin and whispered, 'Ah'm thinkin' 'Swain. If yon Japs don't get tae hell out of it

soon I'll no stand much chance again with that big lassie.'

I thought that if the 'big lassie' could have seen and heard him at that moment she would not have slapped his face. As I said earlier, you couldn't help but like Young Murray.

Looking back over the years, I suppose a few grey hairs are a small price to pay for the privilege of having served with a very select band of men of whom Winston Churchill once told Parliament,

'I have often looked for an opportunity of paying tribute to our submarines. There is no branch of His Majesty's forces which in this war have suffered the same proportion of fatal losses as our Submarine Service. It is the most

dangerous of all services. That is perhaps the reason why the First Lord tells me that entry into it is keenly sought by officers and men. I feel sure that the House would wish to testify its gratitude and admiration to our submarine crews for their skill and devotion, which have proved of inestimable value to the life of our country.'

I don't know to this day whether Young Murray came though safely or whether he finished up worrying the Archangel Gabriel as much as he worried the ship's company of HMS Taurus. But I would like to think he reads these few lines and gets as much happiness as I do myself from my memories.

The Royal Navy's first

HM Submarine Torpedo Boat No 1 (Holland 1) off the Isle of Wight in about 1903. She was launched on October 2, 1901 (the birthday of the Royal Navy's submarine service) at Vickers Sons & Maxim, Barrow-in-Furness. Britain's first submarine was lost under tow to the breaker's yard in 1913. She was successfully salvaged in 1982 and is now being refitted and re-equipped at the Royal Navy Submarine Museum, Gosport with the assistance of Vickers and voluntary helpers led by ex-Chief ERA R R McCurrach

It's launch time — US style!

USS Albuquerque (SSN 708) being launched from the Electric Boat Yard on March 13, 1982. Albuquerque, one of the Los Angeles Class of general purpose nuclear attack submarines, is due to be commissioned in 1984 and has the particular capability of co-ordinated operations with surface ships and other units. Reputedly capable of diving to 1,475 ft (450m) these submarines have a top speed in excess of 30 knots and are heavily armed with SUBROC anti-submarine missiles and Mk 48 torpedoes. It is planned, for the future, to fit Tomahawk cruise missiles

The safe arrival of HM Submarine Torpedo Boat No 1 (Holland I) at the Royal Navy Submarine Museum, Gosport after the successful salvage operation in 1982 is a reminder that the Electric Boat Division of General Dynamics (originated by the Irish-American inventor J P Holland as the Holland Torpedo Boat Company in 1893) has led submarine design and construction for 90 years. This USS Florida (SSBN 728) before launching on November 14, 1981 at Groton, Connecticut. (Electric Boat, Photographs and information kindly supplied by L E Holt, General Dynamics Corporation)

Big eats below

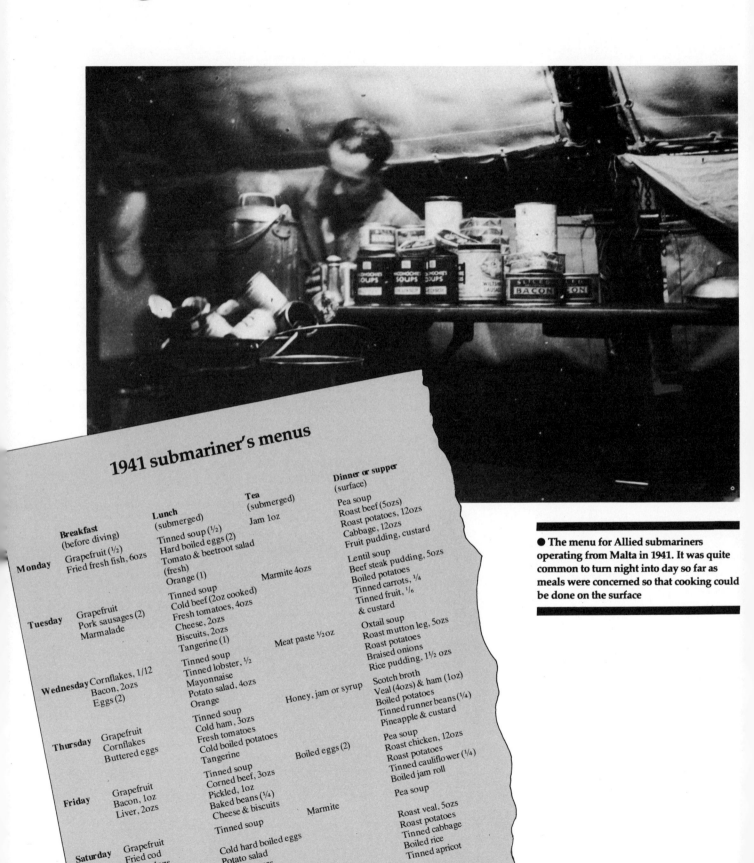

1941 submariner's menus

	Breakfast (before diving)	Lunch (submerged)	Tea (submerged)	Dinner or supper (surface)
Monday	Grapefruit (½) Fried fresh fish, 6ozs	Tinned soup (½) Hard boiled eggs (2) Tomato & beetroot salad (fresh) Orange (1)	Jam 1oz	Pea soup Roast beef (5ozs) Roast potatoes, 12ozs Cabbage, 12ozs Fruit pudding, custard
Tuesday	Grapefruit Pork sausages (2) Marmalade	Tinned soup Cold beef (2oz cooked) Fresh tomatoes, 4ozs Cheese, 2ozs Biscuits, 2ozs Tangerine (1)	Marmite 4ozs	Lentil soup Beef steak pudding, 5ozs Boiled potatoes Tinned carrots, ¼ Tinned fruit, ⅙ & custard
Wednesday	Cornflakes, 1/12 Bacon, 2ozs Eggs (2)	Tinned soup Tinned lobster, ½ Mayonnaise Potato salad, 4ozs Orange	Meat paste ½oz	Oxtail soup Roast mutton leg, 5ozs Roast potatoes Braised onions Rice pudding, 1½ ozs
Thursday	Grapefruit Cornflakes Buttered eggs	Tinned soup Cold ham, 3ozs Fresh tomatoes Cold boiled potatoes Tangerine	Honey, jam or syrup	Scotch broth Veal (4ozs) & ham (1oz) Boiled potatoes Tinned runner beans (¼) Pineapple & custard
Friday	Grapefruit Bacon, 1oz Liver, 2ozs	Tinned soup Corned beef, 3ozs Pickled, 1oz Baked beans (¼) Cheese & biscuits	Boiled eggs (2)	Pea soup Roast chicken, 12ozs Roast potatoes Tinned cauliflower (¼) Boiled jam roll
Saturday	Grapefruit Fried cod fillets, 4ozs	Tinned soup Cold hard boiled eggs Potato salad Tinned pears	Marmite	Pea soup Roast veal, 5ozs Roast potatoes Tinned cabbage Boiled rice Tinned apricot

● The menu for Allied submariners operating from Malta in 1941. It was quite common to turn night into day so far as meals were concerned so that cooking could be done on the surface

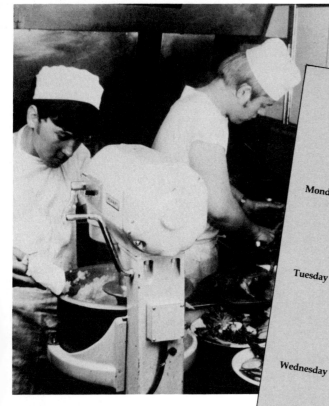

● Above, the galley in HMS Resolution (SSBN) and right a nuclear submarine's menu. Diesel submarines are also generously victualled. There are two cooks in British O-class 'conventional' submarines. In addition to producing meals for a crew of 70 they have to bake fresh bread daily at sea when the initial stock of 600 loaves is exhausted (or mouldy!) after about 10 days at sea. The task is not made easier by the crew having to eat in shifts due to watchkeeping requirements and the chefs are amongst the hardest working men on board. A diesel-electric submarine normally carries food for 10 weeks — about seven tons of provisions including emergency supplies

1983 nuclear submariner's typical menus

	Breakfast	**Lunch**	**Dinner**
Monday	Standard Choice Eggs to order Bacon, sausage, baked beans, tomatoes *plus extra*	Steak & veg. pie Omelettes to order Salad selection Chipped & boiled potatoes Choice of vegetables Fruit flan & custard	Roast lamb & mint sauce Liver & bacon Cottage pie Fondant & creamed potatoes Cabbage, butter beans & peas Cheese & biscuits
Tuesday	Black Pudding Standard choice *plus extra* Fish cakes	Cheesy Hammy Eggy Omelettes to order Salad selection Chipped & boiled potatoes Choice of vegetabls Sultana roll & custard	Boiled silverside & dumplings Sweet & sour pork Rabbit pie Boiled & creamed potatoes Turnips, green beans, broccoli Cheese & biscuits Fresh fruit
Wednesday	Standard choice *plus extra* Saute kidney	Choice of fish dishes Omelettes to order Salad selection Chipped & boiled potatoes Choice of vegetables Chocolate pudding & custard	Roast chicken & stuffing Shepherds pie Pork chops & apple sauce Roast & marquis potatoes Cabbage, carrots & brussels Cheese & biscuits
Thursday	Standard choice *plus extra* Kippers	Pizza pie Omelettes to order Salad selection Chipped & boiled potatoes Choice of vegetables Apple crumble & custard	Baked gammon & peach sauce Braised liver & onions Lamb chop & egg Lyonnaise & baked potatoes BITS, peas & carrots Cheese & biscuits Fresh fruit
Friday	Standard choice *plus extra* Pork luncheon meat fritters	Brown stew & dumplings Omelettes to order Salad selection Chipped & boiled potatoes Choice of vegetables Fruit & ice cream	Grilled & fried steak Cod portions Spaghetti Bolognaise Chipped & creamed potatoes Fried onions, sweetcorn & peas Cheese & biscuits
Saturday	Standard choice *plus extra* Smoked haddock	Cottage pie Omelettes to order Salad selection Sauté & boiled potatoes Choice of vegetables Rice pudding & jam sauce	Chicken pie Savoury mince Gammon steak & pineapple Scallop & creamed potatoes Swede tomatoes & green beans Cheese & biscuits Fresh fruit
Sunday	Standard choice *plus extra* Grapefruit segments Mushrooms	Roast beef & Yorkshire pudding 100% salad Roast turkey & stuffing Roast pork & apple sauce Roast & boiled potatoes Cabbage, carrots & cauliflower Jelly, fruits & cream	Baked potatoes Cheese & biscuits

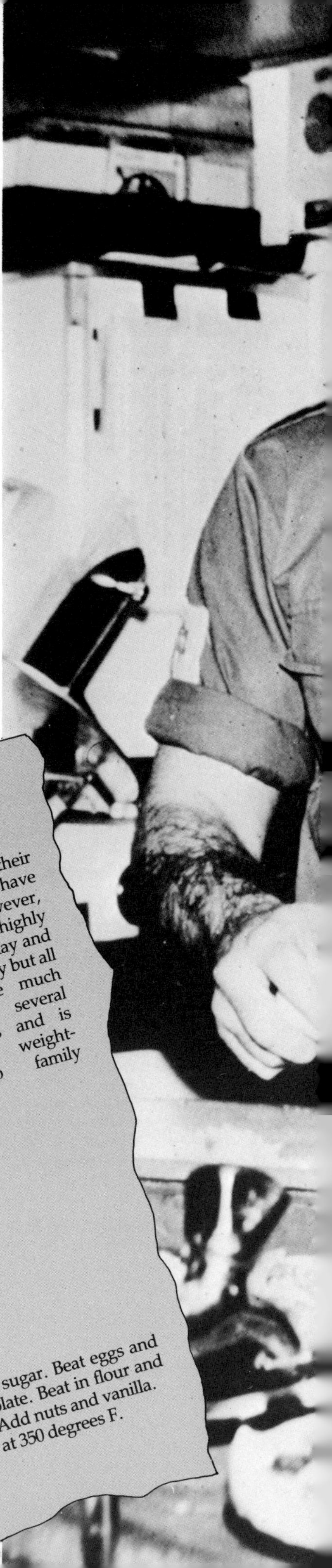

Polaris meals at hotel prices

If the meals were bought ashore in a three star hotel this is what each Polaris meal would cost. Figures kindly supplied by Bryan Goulding, Head of the Hotel and Catering Department, Highbury College of Technology, Portsmouth

	Breakfast	Lunch	Dinner
Monday	£3.75	£4.00	£7.00
Tuesday	£3.75	£4.00	£6.50
Wednesday	£3.75	£4.00	£7.50
Thursday	£3.75	£3.75	£8.20
Friday	£3.75	£4.00	£9.00
Saturday	£3.75	£4.00	£8.20
Sunday	£3.75	£8.00	£5.00
	£26.25	£31.75	£51.40
			£109.40

The standard of messing is very high nowadays for all, especially in nuclear submarines where fresh water and power for cooking is unlimited

Brownies

American submariners, unlike their British counterparts, do not have afternoon tea as a set meal. However, they enjoy a succession of highly calorific snacks throughout the day and night: amongst these, lead-heavy but all too tempting, Brownies are much favoured. This is one of several marginally different recipes and is recommended for non weight-watchers. Reduced to family proportions, you require:

1/4 pound butter
2 eggs
1/2 cup nuts
2/3 cup of flour
Dash baking powder

1 cup sugar
1/4 cup milk
2 1/2 squares chocolate
1/4 teaspoon salt
Vanilla

Cream butter and sugar. Beat eggs and add melted chocolate. Beat in flour and milk alternately. Add nuts and vanilla. Bake 30 minutes at 350 degrees F.

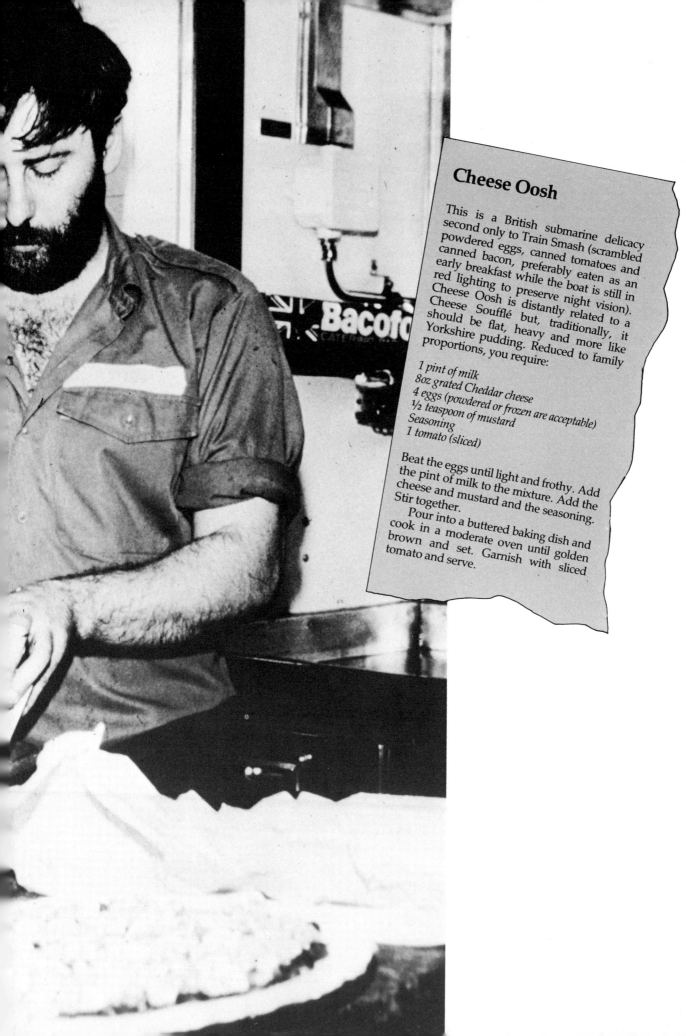

Cheese Oosh

This is a British submarine delicacy second only to Train Smash (scrambled powdered eggs, canned tomatoes and canned bacon, preferably eaten as an early breakfast while the boat is still in red lighting to preserve night vision). Cheese Oosh is distantly related to a Cheese Soufflé but, traditionally, it should be flat, heavy and more like Yorkshire pudding. Reduced to family proportions, you require:

1 pint of milk
8oz grated Cheddar cheese
4 eggs (powdered or frozen are acceptable)
½ teaspoon of mustard
Seasoning
1 tomato (sliced)

Beat the eggs until light and frothy. Add the pint of milk to the mixture. Add the cheese and mustard and the seasoning. Stir together.

Pour into a buttered baking dish and cook in a moderate oven until golden brown and set. Garnish with sliced tomato and serve.

British submarine losses

1900-1914

A1 18.3.1904, Sunk in collision with SS *Berwick Castle*. Subsequently raised, 18.4.1904

A8 1905, Sunk by accident in Plymouth Harbour

C11 14.7.1909, Sunk in collision with SS *Eddystone*

A3 2.2.1912, Sunk in collision with HMS *Hazard*. Raised and sunk again after use as a target, 17.5.1912

B2 4.10.1912, Sunk in collision with SS *Amerika*

A7 16.1.1914, Lost in Whitesand Bay

1914-1918

AE1 19.9.1914, Lost off Bismarck Archipelago

D5 3.10.1914, Sunk in North Sea

E3 18.10.1914, Sunk in North Sea

D2 25.11.1914, Sunk in North Sea

C31 4.1.1915, Lost off Belgian coast

E10 18.1.1915, Sunk in North Sea

E15 15.4.1915, Wrecked in Dardanelles

AE2 30.4.1915, Sunk in Sea of Marmara

C33 4.8.1915, Sunk in North Sea

E13 18.8.1915, Wrecked off Saltholm

C29 29.8.1915, Sunk in North Sea

E7 4.9.1915, Sunk in Dardanelles

E20 6.11.1915, Sunk in Sea of Marmara

E6 26.12.1915, Sunk in North Sea

E17 6.1.1916, Wrecked on Dutch coast

H6 18.1.1916, Wrecked on Dutch coast

E5 7.3.1916, Sunk in North Sea

E24 24.3.1916, Sunk in North Sea

E22 25.4.1916, Sunk in North Sea

E18 24.5.1916, Sunk in Baltic

E26 6.7.1916, Sunk in North Sea

H3 15.7.1916, Sunk in Adriatic

B10 9.8.1916, Sunk by aircraft at Venice

E16 22.8.1916, Sunk in North Sea

E30 22.11.1916, Sunk in North Sea

E37 1.12.1916, Sunk in North Sea

Between March 1904 and September 1983 altogether 156 British submarines have been lost. In a few instances they have been raised and recommissioned

E36 19.1.1917, Sunk in North Sea

E49 12.3.1917, Sunk off Shetland Islands

C34 21.7.1917, Sunk off Shetland Islands

E47 20.8.1917, Sunk in North Sea

G9 16.9.1917, Sunk by accident in North Sea

C32 24.10.1917, Wrecked in Baltic

K1 18.11.1917, Sunk in collision in North Sea

H5 6.1.1918, Sunk in collision in Irish Sea

G8 14.1.1918, Sunk in North Sea

H10 19.1.1918, Sunk in North Sea

E14 28.1.1918, Sunk in Dardanelles

K4 31.1.1918, Sunk in collision off May Island

K17 31.1.1918, Sunk in collision off May Island

E50 31.1.1918, Sunk in North Sea

D3 15.3.1918, Sunk by accident in English Channel

E1
E8
E9
E19   } 3.4.1918. Destroyed in Baltic to avoid capture
C26
C27
C35

C3 23.4.1918, Blown up at Zeebrugge

D6 28.6.1918, Sunk off Ireland

E34 20.7.1918, Sunk in North Sea

L10 3.10.1918, Sunk in North Sea

J6 15 10.1918, Sunk by accident in North Sea

G7 1.11.1918, Sunk in North Sea

1918-1939

G11 22.11.1918, Sunk by accident off Howick

L55 9.6.1919, Sunk in Baltic by Bolsheviks

K5 20.1.1921, Sunk during manoeuvres in Bay of Biscay

H42 23.3.1922, Sunk in collision with HMS *Versatile*

L24 10.1.1924, Sunk in collision with HMS *Resolution*

M1 12.11.1925, Sunk in collision with SS *Vidar*

H29 9.8.1926, Sunk by accident at Devonport

H47 9.7.1929, Sunk in collision with L12 in Irish Sea

Poseidon 9.6.1931, Sunk in collision with SS *Yuta*, China

M2 26.1.1932, Sunk by accident in English Channel

Thetis 1.6.1939, Sunk during trials in Liverpool Bay. Raised and renamed *Thunderbolt*

1939-1945

Oxley 10.9.1939, Sunk by accident off Norway

Seahorse 7.1.1940, Sunk in North Sea

Undine 7.1.1940, Sunk in North Sea

Starfish 9.1.1940, Sunk in North Sea

Thistle 10.4.1940, Sunk off Norway

Tarpon 14.4.1940, Sunk in North Sea

Sterlet 18.4.1940, Sunk in Skagerrak

Unity 29.4.1940, Sunk in collision in North Sea

Seal 5.5.1940, Surrendered in Kattegat

Odin 14.6.1940, Sunk in Mediterranean

Grampus 24.6.1940, Sunk in Mediterranean

Orpheus 27.6.1940, Sunk in Mediterranean

Shark 6.7.1940, Sunk off Norway

Salmon 9.7.1940, Sunk off Norway

Phoenix 17.7.1940, Sunk in Mediterranean

Thames 23.7.1940, Sunk off Norway

Narwhal 1.8.1940, Sunk off Norway

Oswald 1.8.1940, Sunk in Mediterranean

Spearfish 1.8.1940, Sunk off Norway

H49, 18.10.1940, Sunk in North Sea

Rainbow 19.10.1940, Sunk in Mediterranean

Triad 20.10.1940, Sunk in Mediterranean

Swordfish 16.11.1940, Sunk in Bay of Biscay

Regulus 6.12.1940, Sunk in Mediterranean

Triton 18.12.1940, Sunk in Mediterranean

Snapper 12.2.1941, Sunk in Bay of Biscay

Usk 3.5.1941, Sunk in Mediterranean

Undaunted 13.5.1941, Sunk in Mediterranean

Umpire 19.7.1941, Sunk in collision in North Sea

Union 22.7.1941, Sunk in Mediterranean

Cachalot 4.8.1941, Sunk in Mediterranean

P33 20.8.1941, Sunk in Mediterranean

P32 23.8.1941, Sunk in Mediterranean

Tetrarch 2.11.1941, Sunk in Mediterranean

Perseus 1.12.1941, Sunk in Mediterranean

H31 24.12.1941, Sunk in Bay of Biscay

Triumph 20.1.1942, Sunk in Mediterranean

Tempest 13.2.1942, Sunk in Mediterranean

P38 25.2.1942, Sunk in Mediterranean

P39 26.3.1942, Sunk by aircraft at Malta

P36 1.4.1942, Sunk by aircraft at Malta

Pandora 1.4.1942, Sunk by aircraft at Malta

Upholder 14.4.1942, Sunk in Mediterranean

Urge 6.5.1942, Sunk in Mediterranean

Olympus 8.5.1942, Sunk in Mediterranean

P514 21.6.1942, Sunk by accident in Atlantic

Thorn 6.8.1942, Sunk in Mediterranean

Talisman 18.9.1942, Sunk in Mediterranean

Unique 24.10.1942, Sunk in Atlantic

Unbeaten 11.11.1942, Sunk in Bay of Biscay

Utmost 24.11.1942, Sunk in Mediterranean

P222 12.12.1942, Sunk in Mediterranean

Traveller 12.12.1942, Sunk in Mediterranean

P48 25.12.1942, Sunk in Mediterranean

P311 8.1.1943, Sunk in Mediterranean

Vandal 24.2.1943, Sunk in accident in Firth of Clyde

Tigris 10.3.1943, Sunk in Mediterranean

Thunderbolt 13.3.1943, Sunk in Mediterranean (ex-*Thetis*)

Turbulent 23.3.1943, Sunk in Mediterranean

Regent 16.4.1943, Sunk in Mediterranean

P615 18.4.1943, Sunk off West Africa

Splendid 21.4.1943, Sunk in Mediterranean

Sahib 24.4.1943, Sunk in Mediterranean

Untamed 30.5.1943, Sunk during exercises off Scotland

Parthian 11.8.1943, Sunk in Mediterranean

Saracen 18.8.1943, Sunk in Mediterranean

X9 16.9.1943, Lost under tow to *Tirpitz*

X8 18.9.1943, Lost under tow to *Tirpitz*

X5 22.9.1943 (presumed), Lost in attack on *Tirpitz*

X6 22.9.1943, Lost in attack on *Tirpitz*

X7 22.9.1943, Lost in attack on *Tirpitz*

X10 3.10.1943, Scuttled after attempt on *Tirpitz*

Usurper 11.10.1943, Sunk in Mediterranean

Trooper 17.10.1943, Sunk in Mediterranean

Simoon 19.11.1943, Sunk in Mediterranean

X22 7.2.1944, Sunk in collision in Pentland Firth

Graph 20.3.1944, Wrecked on coast of Scotland

Stonehenge 22.3.1944, Sunk in Indian Ocean

Syrtis 28.3.1944, Sunk of Norway

Sickle 18,6,1944, Sunk in Mediterranean

Stratagem 22.11.1944, Sunk in Indian Ocean

Porpoise 19.1.1945, Sunk in Indian Ocean

1945-1983

Truculent 12.1.1950, Sunk in collision with MV *Divina*

Affray 17.4.1951, Sunk by accident in English Channel

Sidon 16.6.1955, Foundered alongside depot ship, Portland, following internal HTP torpedo explosion.

81

Escape from submarines

SUBMARINE ESCAPE is not a popular subject with the public (except when disaster strikes) and is largely ignored by submariners themselves. Why? From the earliest days thoughts of escape have been shunned by submariners because accidents are mostly fatal so why clutter up the submarine with gear you can never use? Nor were the escape methods and equipment trusted; and it is clear now that this distrust was well-founded because most were downright dangerous in any but the shallowest water.

Escape enthusiasm was further reduced by the fact that, although a submarine is built to survive great depths, the bulkheads which subdivide it are puny by comparison. A submarine built to withstand 500 feet with a healthy safety factor in reserve might have watertight bulkheads to withstand only 100 feet. Usually a submarine must be flooding uncontrollably to be sinking at all, so unless the crew can retire behind a good pressure-tight bulkhead, there will be no survivors left to bother about escaping. Thus, with submarines built before the 1950's, there was little need to think about deep escape.

But in 1961 the Royal Navy undertook escape gear trials to 260 feet. Free ascent using only a life-jacket needed a cool head, courage and determination and the trial underlined the need for further research in the submarines which would be at sea from the 1960's onwards, the *Porpoise* class, whose bulkheads were good for 500 feet.

So, in 1963 we started shore trials to see how far the human frame could go without damage underwater. The old oxygen re-breathing escape sets had already been discarded; escape was achieved by flooding the submarine to balance the pressure on both sides of the escape hatch, taking a deep breath and floating to the surface by lifebelt. If the escaper fills his lungs at, say, 250 feet, he will have a pressure in them of about 115 lbs per square inch — not that he will

● by Matthew Todd. Lieutenant-Commander M R Todd was the RN's Submarine Command Escape Diving Officer from 1965 to 1972. He pioneered three escapes from great depths and was awarded the MBE in 1970, having been elected the Navy's Man of the Year in 1969. Several navies have since adopted the system developed in the Royal Navy and they come to England to practice escape drills in the 100-foot escape tower at HMS Dolphin, Fort Blockhouse, the alma mater of British submarines

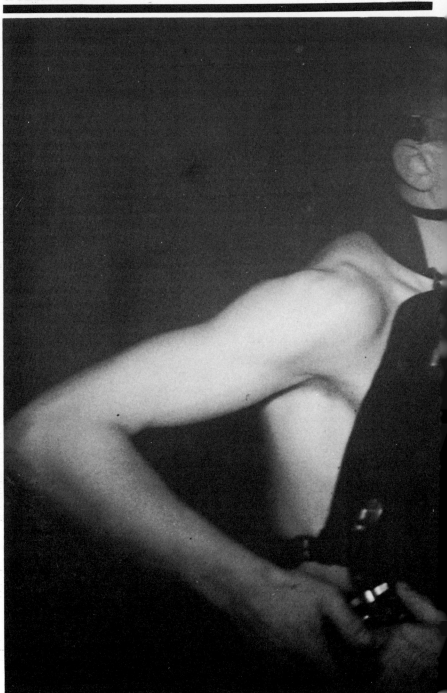

Practising with a DSEA set in the shallow training tank at HMS Dolphin, 1942

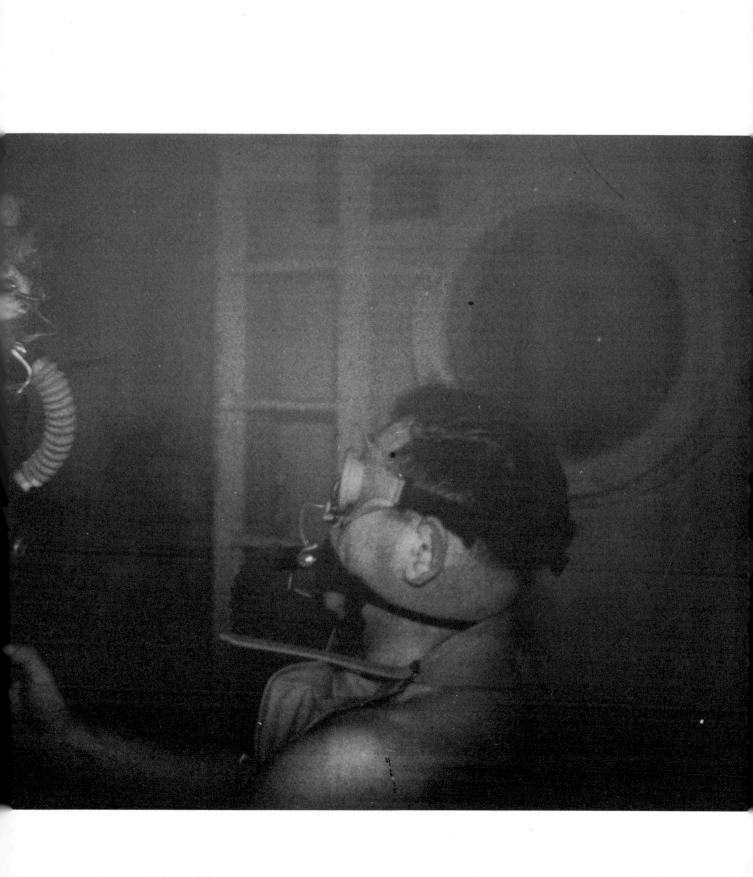

notice, because the pressure around him is the same but, as he ascends, so the pressure on him will reduce, eventually to the pressure at the surface. Now, if he holds his breath, as most people do instinctively, he will arrive at the surface with 115 lbs per square inch in his lungs which could never happen, as his lungs would have burst long before. So men had to be taught how to breathe out continually on the way up without killing themselves.

There are other dangers. If a man breathes in an increasing pressure extra gases will be dissolved first in his bloodstream and then in his tissues until saturation is reached. Remove that pressure quickly, as in an escape, and the extra gases come out of solution as bubbles. This is a grossly simple description of the usual 'bend' or decompression sickness. If a man stops at 300 feet for more than three minutes he is likely to get a bend if he surfaces directly from there. Add to this the fact that the nitrogen in the air we breathe becomes more narcotic the higher the pressure, and that oxygen becomes toxic at high pressure, and you have the measure of the problem of deep escape.

In 1963 we aimed for 500 feet knowing that at this level nitrogen narcosis could be complete enough to prevent the escape, and we would be well inside oxygen poisoning country. However, each of these potential killers required time to take effect so, if we could balance the pressure on the escaper with that of the sea quickly enough, and despatch him to the surface without delay, he might dodge them all.

By totally ignoring diving practice we discovered that man can survive what were previously thought to be catastrophic pressure changes. In pressure terms, we could go from 1 Atmosphere (surface) to 16 Atmospheres (500 feet) in 16 seconds, where a diver would take nearly five minutes. The time spent at depth had to be less than 50 seconds, otherwise a direct ascent to the surface would cause bends. Oxygen poisoning takes a little longer so, in avoiding bends, we had also sidestepped oxygen convulsions. And in the event nitrogen narcosis did not intrude noticeably.

Now it remained only to design a means of despatching the escaper in less than 50 seconds. A tall order but feasible. We concentrated on this. As a submariner, he has little experience of being underwater like a diver. He may be frightened, even stupid; but must still be able to escape. Much thought and many experiments developed equipment which made this startling and unnatural experience quite enjoyable and even fun.

The escaper dons the immersion suit which, later, will protect him on the surface. He zip-fastens a hood with a visor over his head and climbs into the Single Escape Tower built on to the top of the submarine, one at each end. By plugging a large connector attached to his left wrist into a simple socket air is supplied, inflating a built-in lifejacket and overflowing into his hood. Sea pressure is then applied and, in 16

Free ascent with buoyancy. When the DSEA was withdrawn, Free Ascent took over. As the escape compartment flooded the escaper took a last breath from the BIBS (his exhaled breath had already inflated his lifejacket), ducked under the twill trunk and started his ascent from the now open escape hatch above the trunk. During ascent the pressure on him was reduced and his life depended on breathing out the expanding air in his lungs before it burst them. In an escape from 100 feet (30 metres) he would have to breathe out three lungfuls. The picture shows a man under training arriving at the surface after such an ascent in the Submarine Escape Training Tank, HMS Dolphin. Supervising in the control position is the author

seconds or less, he is ready to leave. The valve supplying him with air has kept his lifejacket and hood topped up all the way so, when the hatch above him opens upwards into the sea, he goes merrily on his way because there is nothing to retard his buoyancy. As he ascends (at eight feet per second) he breathes normally from the air in his hood. In fact, he breathes out more than he breathes in, but he need not know this, so the air in his lungs is at the same pressure as the sea around him all the way to the surface with little danger of burst lungs. On the surface he unzips his hood, inflates his double-skinned suit and waits to be picked up. He has made the journey from One Atmosphere in the submarine at 500 feet to 16 Atmospheres and back to One Atmosphere at the surface, all inside 85 seconds — beating bends, narcosis, convulsions and burst lungs.

In July 1965 this system was proved from a submarine at 500 feet at sea. What was it like? Bursting an eardrum during an actual escape is of no consequence at all and many escapers will be bound to suffer this fairly minor, albeit painful, inconvenience; but in a trial with daily escapes it was unacceptable. Having had difficulty in balancing the pressure on both sides of my own eardrum, this was a constant worry to me in leading the trials team. A momentary relaxation might disbar me from the rest of the work and jeopardise the trials.

The valve providing air in the hood during pressurisation would make the difference between life and death. Its failure at the wrong moment would cause what old-time divers feared — a squeeze — and death; so I kept an (undamaged and attentive!) ear on the sound of it throughout. Now pressure balance would be reached and the top hatch would open. At this point the escaper is on his own of which I was fully conscious!

The sea is dark — more so, seemingly, because the escape tower is bright — and there I am, alone, with something like 500 feet to go, the submarine, unseeing, somewhere below. If the hood bursts I will have to revert, immediately, to the old-fashioned ascent, breathing deliberately and continually into the sea throughout that long journey upwards, since a lot of my buoyancy will have been lost. If this

85

happens I will have about two minutes to go without taking a breath and will probably have a bend after I arrive because of the extra time under pressure. But, with a cool head, it can be done. So keep cool!

Now the water is lighter. I feather my hands so that I turn slowly as I rise. This gives a better view in case there should be anything to run into. Hitting the surface is exhilarating. Unflurried I unzip the hood and start to look around for the pick-up team.

I run through the whole sequence in my mind to determine whether any oddities had occurred. For instance, during pressurisation the 'horizon' as seen by my eyes swayed about ten degrees either side of the horizontal. This I was well used to and meant little. Itching on the face after an acent was another red-herring and not one of the manifestations of bends . . . oddities perhaps, but in the circumstances, normal.

We had proved the system. More importantly, we had shown it to be safe and simple. Nothing would have discouraged the submariners around us more than extraordinary drills and long, serious faces. As it was, perhaps some of the onlookers thought us a trifle light-hearted and facetious, but that was what we intended.

Five years later we did it again — from 600 feet this time, almost doubling the world's best and making successful escape possible over the Continental shelf. At last submariners had an easy method they could rely on down to the depth where most submarine internal bulkeads would hold together.

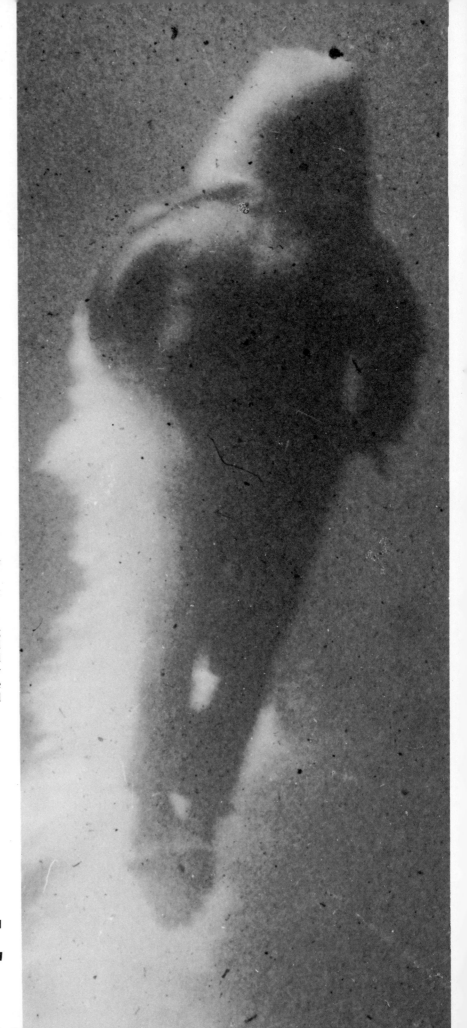

On the way up at speed!

Events and developments in submarine escape

1851
February 1 Wilhelm Bauer's *Sea Diver* collapses and sinks in Kiel roadstead in about 18 metres. Bauer, reputedly with a spanner, persuades his two crew members to flood the submarine in order to equalise pressure and open the hatch, thus becoming the first submariner to realise this prerequisite of escape

1863
Le Plonguer (Bourgeois and Brun) floods through a broken scuttle at seven metres on her first dive at Rochefort. Her crew of 12 escape through a caisson built round her conning tower hatch for this purpose. The caisson was fitted for the trial dive only, and her 12-man escape boat, included in the design, was successfully tested later

1878
Paul Bert (Fr) following work in 1860 by Professor Leroy de Mericourt, suggests Caisson Disease (Diver's Bends) is caused by bubbles of gas (nitrogen) appearing out of solution in the blood and tissues when ambient pressure is lowered rapidly from a high level. He also demonstrates that oxygen at high pressure is toxic, causing convulsions in animals at three or four Atmospheres. (Later knowledge shows clearly that, in fact, convulsions can occur at a much lesser pressure and even at one Atmosphere or 10 metres)

The submarine escape immersion suit (SEIS). Introduced in 1952, seen here with the last of the DSEA, and still in use in a developed form. This was the first purpose-designed protection for escapers in the world; it has a double skin with the space between inflated from a built-in CO_2 bottle after the escaper surfaces. Gloves and a double hood allowed survival for a considerable time even in bad conditions. It was kept stowed on board in small valises in lockers in each escape compartment, enough for all at both ends of the submarine

1902

Simon Lake (USA) makes a trial escape from the diving lock in *Protector* from 10 metres, making a free ascent to the surface. (Simon Lake was a great showman with an eye for the Press)

1904

March 18. *HMS A1* sunk by collision, the first operational submarine to be lost. No lives saved. Serious thought now given to escape and work on the Hall-Rees helmet is started

Two dogs, of mixed ancestry, discharged safely through torpedo tube from USS Shark. Chief Machinist Harry Schaub USN makes a simulated escape from USS Porpoise through the torpedo tube on the surface under the direction of Lieutenant-Commander Fletcher USN, Commandant of Newport Torpedo Station. Conclusion, 'the only danger that is apparent is that with the shock of being discharged from the tube, the man will be temporarily deprived of his breath.'

1905

Korrigan (Fr) remains dived for 12 hours using air purification with no ill effects on crew.

Farfadet (Fr) sinks, trapping 14 men some of whom remain alive for 32 hours during unsuccessful salvage attempts hampered by foul weather. (The boat was salvaged eventually). French submarines of this type had water-tight sub-division

Salvage lifting eyes ordered for fitting on British submarines but cancelled in 1906 because of weight

Wilhelm Bauer's Sea Diver which collapsed on February 1, 1851 and forced the three-man crew to make the first escape. Shown above is the observation turret in Sea Diver

1906
Bonite (Fr) survives collision by releasing drop weights

1908
Air-locks, with 16 Hall-Rees helmets in each (one for each crew member) installed in *HMS C12 - C16*. The helmets and frocks were bulky, unpopular and never used

1909
April 15. Ensign Kenneth Whiting, *USS Porpoise*, swims out of flooded torpedo tube while submarine is surfaced. Rebuked by Chairman of Electric Boat Company who declares venture foolhardy and unnecessary. Undeterred Whiting goes on to make free ascent from tube at eight metres, followed by Midshipman Deem from 12 metres who then made the reverse journey holding his breath — an exploit that unquestionably *was* foolhardy and unnecessary

HMS D1 fitted with an escape tower aft

1910
Professor Haldane designs CO_2 measuring device

The Davis submerged escape apparatus (DSEA), in service in the Royal Navy from 1930 to 1952. The counterlung of rubberised material was supplied with pure oxygen from the bottle underneath it. The wearer breathed through the canister containing soda lime built into the middle of the counterlung, thus removing carbon dioxide as he breathed. Just above the O_2 bottle was an apron to extend forward so that the ascent was slowed; fast ascents were considered to be dangerous during the life of this equipment. On the right is pictured the McCann rescue bell on HMS Seraph for trials in 1952

1911

U3 (Ger) sinks on trials in Kiel Harbour. Most of the crew rescued by salvage vessel *Vulcan*. Telephone buoy and air purification used while awaiting rescue

R H Davis (Brit) designs Oxylithe Breathing Belt. Adopted by USN

1912

German, Swedish and Danish navies adopt Draeger's (Ger) practical and easily stowed oxygen rebreathing escape apparatus

British submarines (E-class) have watertight internal sub-division, making compartment escape at shallow depth a possibility

1913

Russians instal telephone buoys. *Minoga* (Russ) sinks and uses telephone buoy.

Crew rescued by salvage after ten hours

Russians build twin-hulled salvage vessel to lift 1,000 tons from 110 metres. (The Russian Navy, almost from the start, viewed submarine disasters with an air of gloomy inevitability which was fully justified by low morale and poor training)

1913

Cavallini (It) and Gustave Zédé (Fr) build detachable conning towers for escape. Zéde's is later moved forward and called a 'safety cabin'

All French submarines fitted with lifting lugs, telephone buoys and drop-weights. (French submarines were undoubtedly accident-prone as were British boats with the difference that most accidents and disasters in the RN were caused by strenuous efforts to maximise operational effectiveness thereby sometimes exceeding safe

tactical and material limits while experimenting with new procedures. The USN enjoyed remarkably accident-free submarine development)

1916

U51 (Ger) torpedoed in 30 metres. Draeger sets used for the first time: five men escape but two die subsequently

HMS E41 rammed and sunk off Harwich. Stoker PO Brown makes first RN escape using compartment escape and free ascent (depth uncertain, but fairly shallow)

1927

Escape by salvage fails for *USS S4*. Lt Momsen USN directed to investigate methods of individual escape; Lieutenant-Commander McCann looks into collective escape. 'Momsen Lung' and 'McCann Rescue Bell' result

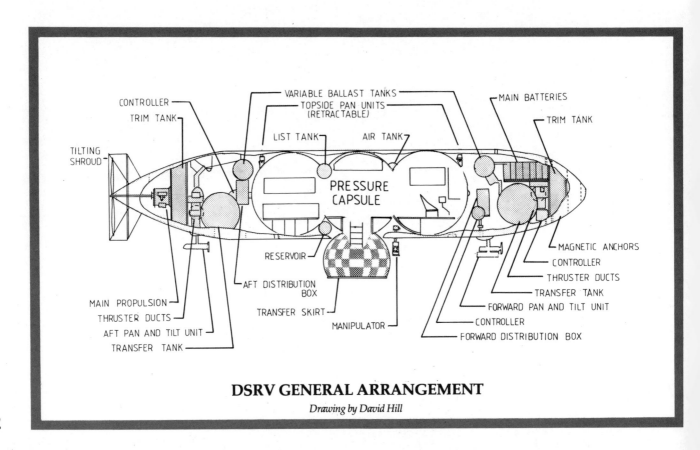

DSRV GENERAL ARRANGEMENT

Drawing by David Hill

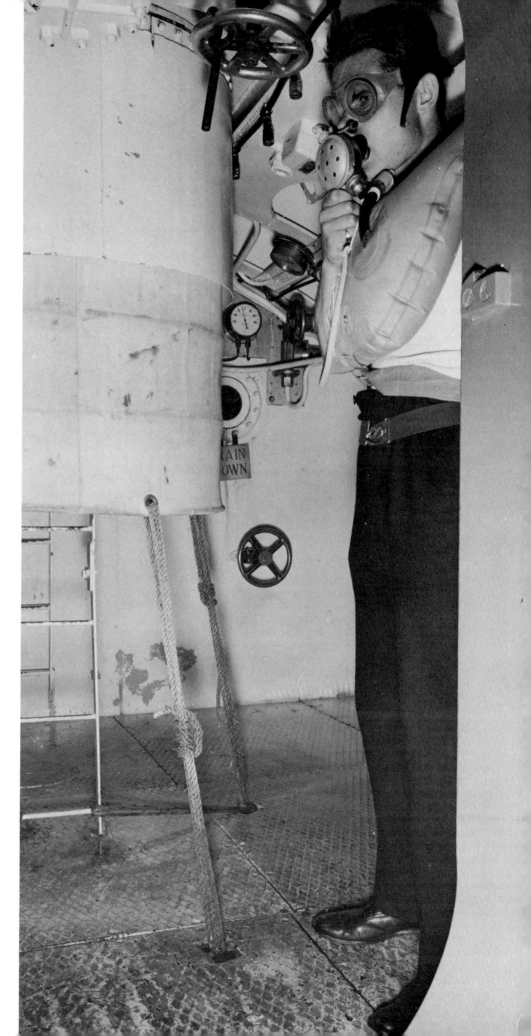

1928

Momsen Lung, with external oxygen supply from manifold in submarine, adopted by USN

1929

Davis Submerged Escape Apparatus (DSEA) adopted by RN. First special escape hatches by now fitted in British *Oberon*-class

Escape training Tank built at *HMS Dolphin* (Fort Blockhouse), four feet deep (1.2 metres)

1930

30 foot (9.1 metres) Escape Training Tank built at *HMSDolphin*

1931

June. Using DSEA, five survive from *HMS Poseidon*, rammed and sunk in 135 metres in China Sea. Two suffer bends

1939

May. *USS Squalus* sinks off New Hampshire. Thirty-three men saved with McCann Rescue Bell

June. *HMS Thetis* sinks in Liverpool Bay through torpedo tube rear door being opened with bow cap open. Four men escape from after compartment using DSEA but 99 men fail to leave submarine (despite part of the hull breaking surface) and perish. War prevents all recommendations from resulting enquiry being implemented

Drop keels discarded in RN because of possible inadvertent release under depth-charge attack

Escaper in the mid-1950s, using the Built-in Breathing System (BIBS) while waiting in the 'submarine' section at the bottom of the 100 ft training tank at HMS Dolphin before flooding up and ducking under the twill trunk

1941
Russians introduce a hood to accompany existing oxygen rebreathing apparatus

1943
British state 100 feet (30 metres) to be maximum safe for DSEA escapes with any real hope of survival but investigate deeper depths with air mixture: goats and, later, human volunteers survive in compression chamber trials from 300 feet (91 metres) equivalent

CO_2 absorption units start to be fitted in submarines both for operational use during prolonged wartime dives and for reducing CO_2 content while awaiting escape

In the USA Momsen, with oxygen apparatus, had successfully demonstrated hand-over-hand ascent up a line from 63 metres

1951
Built-in Breathing System (BIBS) installed in British submarines using 60% oxygen/40% nitrogen mixture

1952
100 foot (30 metres) Escape Training Tower built at *HMS Dolphin* and subsequently used by several navies. Buoyant ascent (no breathing apparatus) training started and Submarine Escape Immersion Suits (SEIS) issued

DSRV Avalon arriving at Glasgow airport, May 1979

1953
Steinke hood (without oxygen or air bottle) in service in USN

1954
BIBS mixture changed to pure air

1960
Commander George Bond USN escapes from submerged submarine at 94 metres during successful deep trials

1962
Twenty-five pairs of men (led by Lieutenant-Commander L D Hamlyn) 'escape' from *HMS Tiptoe* at depths down to 82 metres using buoyant or hooded methods without escape apparatus. Prototype hood (bucket-over-the-head principle) developed to ensure air is available for breathing during compression phase and subsequent ascent

1964
HMS Orpheus escape trials (Lieutenant-Commander M Todd and team) down to 60 metres using prototype Single Escape Tower (SET) and Hooded Immersion Suit (HIS)

1965
1964 trials repeated down to 152 metres (Lt Cdr Todd and team)

1966
British submarines equipped with SET and HIS

1970
January 24. *DSRV1* (USN) launched at San Diego

HMS Osiris escape trials down to 183 metres (Lt Cdr Todd and team)

1978
February 3. *DSRV1* by now named *Mystic*, accepted into the USN Fleet with Submarine Development Group 1, San Diego. *DSRV2, Avalon* follows

September. Transport demonstrated by air-lifting Mystic from San Diego to Providence, Rhode Island, trucking to USN Submarine Base Groton, Connecticut and loading on board *USS Bergall* (SSN 667). Simulated rescue conducted between mother submarine and inert plate on seabed. DSRV total project reputed to cost about $160 million

1979

DSRV Avalon flown to Glasgow, taken by trailer to RN Submarine Base, Faslane and lifted on board *HMS Repulse* (SSBN acting as mother submarine). *HMS Odin* (SSK) simulates distressed submarine and bottoms at 122 metres for Exercise *Latent*, the first DSRV mission to a live bottomed submarine. Commander B O Forbes, OBE, RN, leading the British team claims a record for diving in Vickers lock-out commercial submersible *L1*, transferring first to *Odin*, then to *DSRV Avalon*, and finally to *Repulse* before surfacing!

1982

August 20-28. Exercise *Sedgemore* repeats 1979 operation with *HMS Oppossum* (SSK), well named for playing dead, and *HMS Revenge* (SSBN) as mother submarine

DSRV Avalon on board HMS Repulse (SSBN) acting as MOSUB (Mother Submarine) for exercise Latent, 1979

Flank's flied flippers

● by Richard Compton-Hall

IT HAPPENED between the wars in China where all the best submarine stories came from and where a surgeon lieutenant's life in the depot ship was one long Chinese swan. His Majesty's Submarine *L72* was lying in luxury at Wei-Hei-Wei — the beloved base of submariners and hangers-on between the wars. *L72* was by no means the boldest boat in the flotilla, but she had had a busy life with several bumps on the bottom and a few involuntary excursions to a depth well below her inclinations.

Like most ladies of a certain age she was sensitive about her appearance which had not improved with time. Thus, when the latest in her long line of commanding officers found a double-decker spotter place from the Cruiser Squadron circling above on his way out to the submarine exercise area one morning he would have liked to have drawn an all-concealing veil. But it was too shallow to dive; and as the spotter plane, itself a piece of old Ming, circled ever closer he and others on the bridge could not escape the melody that burst forth from an ancient gramophone mounted on the fuselage in front of the observer and evidently connected to a new-fangled but efficient amplifier, *Any old iron*'.

The Captain was ambitious. If he made a fuss about the insult the Admiral commanding the Cruiser Squadron might take it badly; so, being a card-carrying Christian, he decided to turn the other cheek and gain glory in another way. Despite earnest and loyal remonstrances from his officers he announced his intention of showing that the submarine service could take a joke, especially *L72*. He told the First Lieutenant to organise a dinner party on board, on return to harbour, for the Admiral of the Cruiser Squadron, the Admiral's wife and the pilot and observer of the spotting place. A shrewd move doomed to failure by the eager-to-please Chinese steward appointed, as was customary, to every boat while on the China station.

The steward was an amiable young man with an unpronounceable name. However, a submarine steward anywhere was (and still is) known as 'the Flunk' and since he had already been given the friendly soubriquet of Frank he became, with the usual Chinese inability to pronounce his Rs, 'Flank the Flunk'.

Flank the Flunk announced he would produce a 'velly special dinner with shark flippers in soy sauce'. He knew where shark flippers could be found when they had fallen off the back of a lickshaw . . . The officers got the message and agreed that Flank the Flunk should go ahead and take a careful look at what dropped out of rickshaws. Funds were low.

The dinner was truly magnificent. Flank the Flunk himself was so gratified by the applause, when he appeared with the *pièce de résistance*, that he carried uneaten portions of shark's flipper to the senior rates' mess where the Chief Stoker's pet white rat lived in style in a cupboard originally intended for engineering manuals. Flank held the Chief Stoker and his rat in awe and reverence.

It was about the time that coffee was being served when the Chief Stoker returned from a heavy run ashore to find his rat flat on its back with all four feet in the air. The corpse was already stiffening. Flank the Flunk was almost as petrified as the rat. He had fed it with shark flippers and there was the Admilal and Missy Admilal and the Captain and the rest allee b'long same ploblem. Velly selious.

Blavely, he approached the Captain in the wardroom. The party was in full

swing. The Captain did not at first believe what he had heard. But when the rat was produced it was clear that the lickshaw which the flippers had fallen off was very bad joss. With diffidence the Captain informed the assembled company of the unfortunate circumstances . . .

The Surgeon Lieutenant in the depot ship was delighted. He had had nothing better than an ingrown toenail to deal with for seven weeks and his polo pony was having a month's stand off. Delving deep into a pile of unused medical stores he eventually uncovered a Mark I Stomach Pump that had quite possibly not seen service since the Crimean War with Florence Nightingale at the business end.

The rest of the story is best glossed over. It was not one of those evenings that really end up well.

The Captain was sitting in the wardroom the following morning with a large cup of black coffee and a feeling of emptiness and insecurity when Flank the Flunk burst through the curtained doorway.

'Allee well master,' he beamed. 'The Chief Stoker lat not die flom bad fish. Shark flipper *allee light*. Chief Stoker lat walk acloss electic switchboard. Join ancestors. Chief Electlician find lat and lay out with levelence leady for bulial.'

There were various degrees of security classification in the Royal Navy — Top Security, Secret, Confidential and Medical-in-Confidence. The Captain decided, with an admirable lack of hesitation, to enforce the latter.

HMS L4 (not the subject of this story) on the China station at Wei-Hei-Wei with the Commander-in-Chief on board, 1924. For submariners, between the wars, China was the Lotus land

Underwater sound and the submarine

THE FIELD of underwater acoustics has become of increasing importance as man explores the 'last frontier' — the sea. Currently, underwater sound is used to determine the ocean's depths; locate schools of fish; investigate marine life; explore the ocean's bottoms in search of oil, gas, minerals and gems; detect underground explosions and earthquakes; permit submarines to travel under ice and even to surface in holes in the ice or polynyas (the Russian word). In addition, the military application for detection, classification and localization of submarines has become one of the more important defence efforts in view of the size and increased capabilities of the Soviet submarine force.

The uses of underwater sound constitute the engineering science of *sonar*, and the systems employing underwater sound in one way or another are sonar systems. The word 'sonar' was coined late in World War II as a counterpart of the word 'radar' and came into use later only after having been dignified as an acronym for Sound, Navigation and Ranging.

There are two basic types of sonar systems: passive or listening, and active. A passive sonar system relies simply on the detection of noise generated by the target (Figure 1). An active sonar system, in contrast, requires a sound generator combined with an under-water microphone (hydrophone) which receives the reflected sound waves and converts the sound into electricity (Figure 2). An active sonar system operates in the sea much like an ordinary radar does in the atmosphere.

As with so many other scientific achievements that have resulted in the enhancement of our lives, the major breakthroughs in underwater acoustics have come about as a result of the research and development sponsored for military applications.

Records indicate that there was interest in sounds in the ocean at the time of Aristotle around 350 BC. One of the first references to the use of a listening device in water may be found in the notebooks of Leonardo da Vinci who, in 1483, wrote, 'If you let your ship stop and dip the end of a long blowpipe in the water and hold the other end to your ear, then you can hear ships which are very distant from you.' Although this early example of a passive sonar

● by R Craig Olson, PhD a retired Commander of the USN who spent 17 of the 25 years of his naval career in the submarine service, where he had command of the USS Hardhead (SS 365) and served on the staff of Submarine Development Group Two in New London, Connecticut. After his retirement, he was Head, Sonar Systems Interfaces Division at the David W Taylor Naval Ship Research and Development Center in Bethesda, Maryland. Currently, Dr Olson is a research scientist with Mar Associates Inc where he specializes in research in underwater acoustics, pattern recognition and artificial intelligence

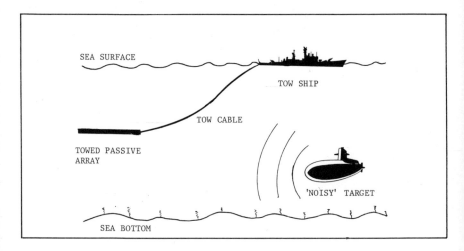

Figure 1 Passive sonar system

system has the merit of extreme simplicity, it does not provide any indication of direction and is insensitive as a result of the great mis-match between acoustic properties of air and water.

There was little improvement to Leonardo's simple listening device until World War I when the damage German submarines inflicted upon Allied shipping was severe. By 1915, after searching for methods to detect submerged submarines, scientists determined that sound is the only form of energy which experiences minimal losses as it travels through the ocean, and that the use of other techniques was unsuitable for submerged submarine detection at distances of more than a few hundred metres. Thus, considerable research and development efforts were

made in the field of underwater acoustics in the UK, France and later in the USA. Two passive sonar systems resulted from this in the UK: a hydrophone (carbon-granule microphone), equipped with a baffle which when suspended from a drifting fishing boat (a very silent platform) provided a bearing and 'estimated' range on a submerged submarine (Figures 3 and 4); and a binaural air-tube listening device which consisted of two tubes and a stethoscope. This later direct listening device was the mainstay of World War I submarine detection capabilities. Some 300 assorted escort craft were eventually fitted with these listening tubes.

World War I submarines were noisy enough to permit these early listening systems to be effective for a large percentage of the time. The listening

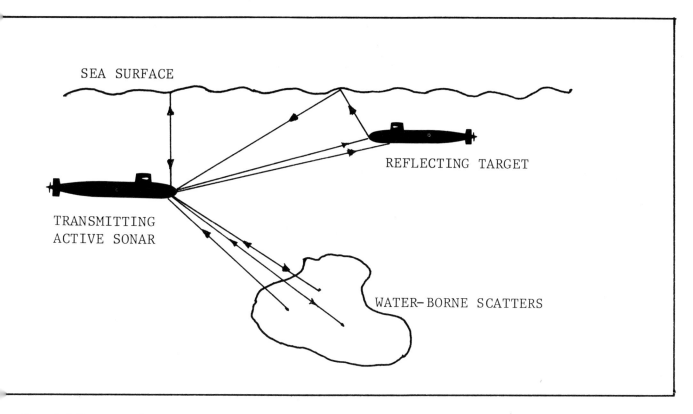

SEA SURFACE

REFLECTING TARGET

TRANSMITTING
ACTIVE SONAR

WATER-BORNE SCATTERS

Figure 2 Active sonar system

systems' performance, however, was often reduced by a submarine which was able to decrease its noise output by running deep at low speed. Thus, a need was established to develop a different type of sonar system, one which, by generating its own sound source, could detect even a completely silent submarine by listening for return echoes, ie, an 'active' sonar system. The idea that 'echo ranging' could be used for submarine detection is attributed to a perceptive Russian engineer, Constantin Chilowksy. Chilowsky worked with the French physicist, P Langevin, to develop an underwater source that transmitted sound across the Seine river in Paris during the winter of 1915-16. Langevin designed an electrostatic sound generator, which was simply a large capacitor with one plate next to the

water. As the electric charge on the second plate was varied, the electric field between the two condenser plates varied causing a variable force on the water place. The water plate was mechanically designed to move with the force variation of the electric field thus creating a sound wave in the adjacent water. The British initiated efforts in active sonar development and, by the summer of 1916, had duplicated the French success. A major step forward was made when Langevin used as his sound source a 'sandwich' comprised of a single plate of specially designed piezoelectric material, quartz, between two plates of steel. The relatively high intensities of this sound generator enabled a two-way transmission under ideal condition to a range of eight kilometres and produced the first

detection of an echo from a submarine.

This quartz crystal echo-ranging system was developed further during the period between the two world wars. Major emphasis was placed upon the development of active sonar in both the US and the USA, although the effort in both nations was limited by restricted naval budgets.

During World War II, further intensive development of echo-ranging techniques was undertaken in the UK and the USA. One of the problems with echo-ranging sonar as it existed in 1941 was that it could cover only a narrow angle, approximately 20 degrees, on each transmission. Typical extreme ranges were less than three kilometres. At these ranges the sound required four seconds to travel to the submarine and back. To make a complete search around

Figure 3 'Drifter set' hydrophone

the ship required about four minutes. To overcome this slow-search problem, a rapid scanning sonar was developed but it was not available for fleet use until after the end of the war.

In addition, operational experience disclosed that the ocean was not an ideal acoustic medium. Sound transmission through the sea was subject to the vagaries of *reflection* (from the ocean boundaries), from *refraction* (from temperature, salinity and pressure variation), from *attenuation* (due to spreading and absorption) as well as other factors. The 'Nature of underwater sound' — discussed in the next section — gradually has evolved from an 'art' in the 1940's to more of a 'science' at the present time.

Nature of underwater sound

For underwater sound the attenuation, that is the loss per unit distance of travel due to absorption and scattering, is far less than the attenuation for underwater light and radio waves. The propagation of low-frequency underwater sound compares favourably with propagation of radio waves in the air. The attenuation for underwater sound at the low audio frequencies is small. In experiments conducted in 1960, sound waves generated by a small explosive charge detonated south of Australia were received off Bermuda after travelling a distance of 21,000 kilometers!

Despite the favourable propagation at the low audio frequencies, there are two serious problems with underwater sound:

Low Propagation Speed. Underwater sound travels at only 1,463 metres per second as compared to the speed of radio waves propagation of 186,000 nautical miles per second in the atmosphere

Attenuation. The attenuation of underwater sound rapidly increases with an increase in frequency. The attenuation loss per unit distance increases approximately with the square of the frequency

The propagation of sound in the ocean is extremely complex. Since the velocity of sound under water varies with temperature, pressure and salinity, it also varies with depth, position and season of the year. The result is a collection of refractive (bending of acoustic waves due to changes in the

sound velocity as a function of depth or horizontal distance) and reflective (the bending back of acoustic waves due to interaction with the surface and/or the bottom of the ocean) effects that complicate efforts to pinpoint acoustic sources, create several regions of sound transmission in the ocean, and sometimes combine to form acoustic wave guides. These variations in sound velocity under some conditions bend underwater sound waves as much as 15 degrees, so that there is no guarantee that the radiated noise from a submarine will consistently reach a given location in the ocean.

The variation of sound velocity with depth may be depicted as a 'velocity profile'. An idealized deep ocean profile is shown in Figure 5. In general, there are four regions of sound transmission in the open oceans. Just below the surface of the ocean is the 'surface layer' in which the sound velocity is susceptible to daily and local changes due to heating, cooling and wind action. This surface layer extends down to a depth between 50 and 60 metres. Sound transmission ray paths are shown in

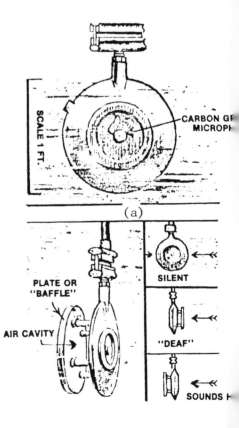

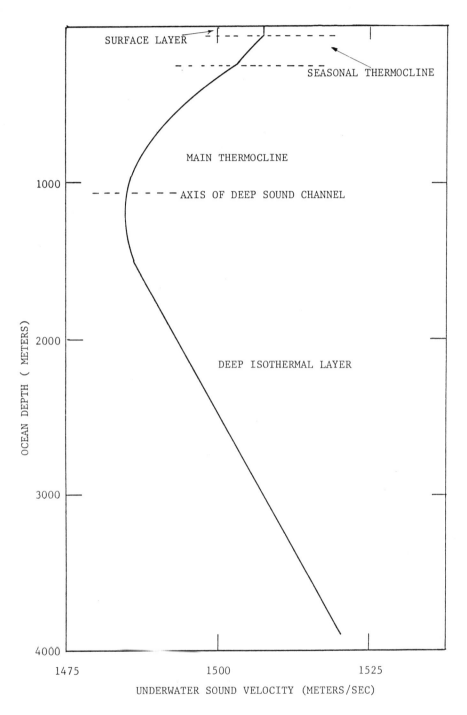

SURFACE LAYER

SEASONAL THERMOCLINE

MAIN THERMOCLINE

AXIS OF DEEP SOUND CHANNEL

DEEP ISOTHERMAL LAYER

1000

2000

3000

4000

OCEAN DEPTH (METERS)

1475   1500   1525

UNDERWATER SOUND VELOCITY (METERS/SEC)

Figure 5 Typical deep-sea velocity profile

Figure 4 Details of 'Drifter set' hydrophone (a) Bidirectional hydrophone (without baffle); (b) Undirectional hydrophone, silent (top right) 'deaf; (middle right), and so sounds are heard (bottom right)

figure 6 for a typical sound velocity profile in the surface layer. In the next region, between 60 and 250 metres, is the 'seasonal thermocline' or 'temperature gradient'. The seasonal thermocline is characterised by a negative thermal or velocity gradient (temperature or velocity decreasing with depth. This thermocline changes depth, moving up and down, as the water temperatures change with the season. The next region, which is immediately below the seasonal thermocline, is the 'main thermocline'. It lies between 250 and 1,000 metres and is unaffected by seasonal changes. In all of the three regions mentioned above, the sound velocity generally decreases with depth. (The exception is in the surface layer where under some conditions the sound velocity may increase with depth.) The decrease which is caused by the dominance of temperature effects reverses below 1,000 metres. In the fourth region, sound travels more rapidly with increasing depth since the water temperature is nearly constant and sound velocity increases with water pressure. This region is called the 'deep isothermal layer'.

The variation in the sound velocity as a function of depth results in refraction of sound. This variation causes two interesting and sometimes useful effects:

Deep Sound Channel. The depth at which the velocity reaches a minimum defines the axis of the deep sound channel. A sound wave generated in this channel remains trapped in it and travels by cylindrical spreading for long distances. The deep sound channel and associated sound transmission ray paths are shown in Figure 7. Minimum sound velocity may occur at a depth between 1,000 and 2,000 metres

Convergent Zones. When a sound ray penetrates the deep isothermal layer, it eventually (if it does not strike the ocean bottom first) is refracted upward and strikes the sea surface, where it is reflected and follows similar paths to a second convergent zone, and then on to subsequent zones (Figure 8). At intervals of 48 - 56 kilometres, narrow zones of high acoustic intensity occur near the surface

Applications

Considerable understanding of the vagaries and complexities of sound

103

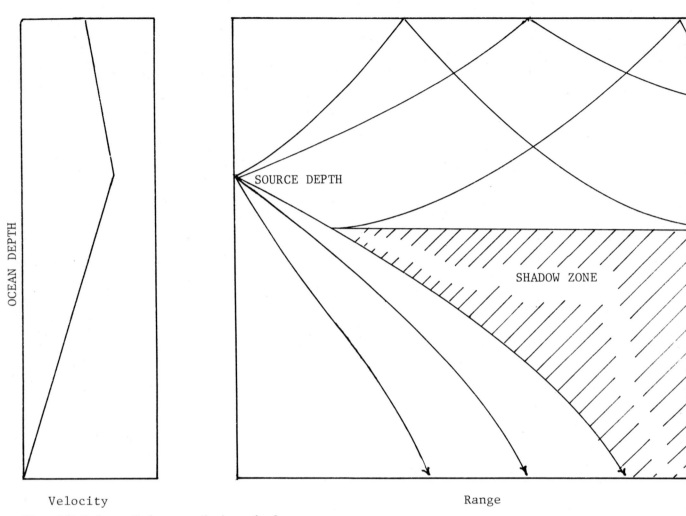

OCEAN DEPTH

SOURCE DEPTH

SHADOW ZONE

Velocity

Range

Figure 6 Typical ray paths for propagation in a surface layer

propagation in the sea was gained between World Wars I and II. Of particular importance was the discovery of the cause of high variability in performance of active sonar performance. Slight thermal gradients were capable of refracting sound deep into the depths of the sea and could cause the submarine to lie in a 'shadow zone'. This situation is shown in the lower part of Figure 6. A device which measures temperature as a function of depth, a bathythermograph, was installed starting in the late 1930's on board all naval vessels engaged in antisubmarine warfare (ASW) tests and operations. The bathythermograph is used as a means to indicate temperature gradients in the upper few hundred metres of the sea. With such information it is possible to determine if shadow zones exist and

thus reduced active sonar can be anticipated.

On both sides of the Atlantic, the World War II period was marked by feverish activity in the field of underwater sound. Most of our present concepts as well as practical applications had their origins in this period. This concentrated effort was undertaken because of the U-boat threat, more effective than in World War I.

After World War II, the development of the nuclear-powered submarine presented major problems. These submarines can remain at sea submerged indefinitely and for very much longer than diesel-electric-powered submarines. Thus complete reliance has to be placed upon underwater acoustics for detection, classification, and localisation functions. Initially, these

submarines that have considerable machinery which must run continuously were noisier than a diesel-electric-powered submarine operating at low speeds on its batteries. A tremendous effort has been made by the USA to silence their nuclear-powered submarines. Soviet nuclear-powered submarines, in contrast, have been and continue to be, comparatively noisy, although the Soviets have instituted silencing programmes of their own. Thus, since the late 1950's, there has been a major effort to develop sonar systems which will use the knowledge of underwater sound propagation and which will provide long distance detection capabilities. Several examples of sonar systems which have been designed, built and are now operational include:

Variable depth sonars Variable depth sonars have been developed and installed in some surface ASW vessels. The sound projector and associated receiver of an active sonar system are towed by cable behind the surface vessels at depths great enough to penetrate thermoclines and thus can provide a capability to detect submarines lying under cover.

Multi-propagation path sonar systems Three basic propagation modes are available to surface ships and submarines: direct, bottom-bounce and convergence zone (Figure 9). Both active and passive sonar systems have been designed for operations in all three modes. These systems are currently being installed both in surface ASW vessels and in submarines. To achieve an active sonar capability to utilise all three propagation modes, the system designers used higher acoustic powers, lower frequencies and advanced signal processing techniques. A capability to search in the vertical (depth) in addition to the horizontal plane also was provided. Similarly, passive sonar systems have tended to migrate to lower frequencies, where both acoustic output of a submarine is greater and attenuation of sound in the sea is less.

Passive towed arrays The sonar system designer had to contend with the increased sonar self-noise levels in both surface ships and submarines when lower frequencies were to be used. One technique to overcome such limitations is to tow a passive acoustic line array astern at sufficient distance where there is minimal system degradation due to tow-ship noise

Fixed bottom-mounted passive sensors Fixed arrays of hydrophones known as the SOSUS (sound surveillance system) have been planted on the floor of the Atlantic and Pacific Oceans. SOSUS takes advantage of the quiet environment and the good propagation conditions at the locations where the hydrophones have been placed. SOSUS is a low frequency and relatively long-range passive system

Conclusion

The advancements in the field of underwater acoustics and in the development of sonar systems have been made in large measure because of the U-boat threat in World Wars I and II,

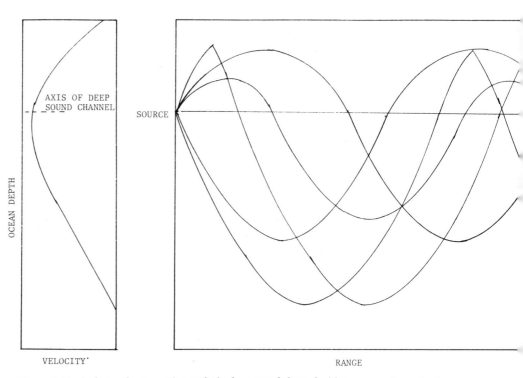

Figure 7 Typical sound propagation paths in deep sound channel with source on channel axis

Figure 8 Typical propagation paths for convergent zone formation with a shallow source

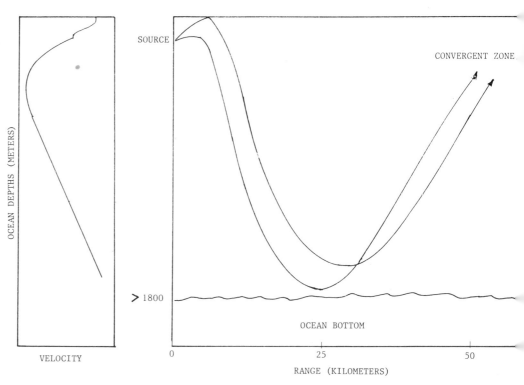

and now by the increased size of the Soviet submarine force. The advent of nuclear-powered submarines that can remain at sea for long periods present a threat which could not have been made by the earlier diesel-electric-powered submarines. As the radiated noises of Soviet submarines decrease, there will be a continual challenge to the underwater acoustician and the sonar system designer to maintain sufficient sonar capabilities. Even though there has been major progress in the field of underwater acoustics in the last 70 years, there is a continued challenge for improvements to be made from a military application standpoint. Also there will be increased demands on this field of science to satisfy man's needs as he explores the seas for commercial and peaceful purposes.

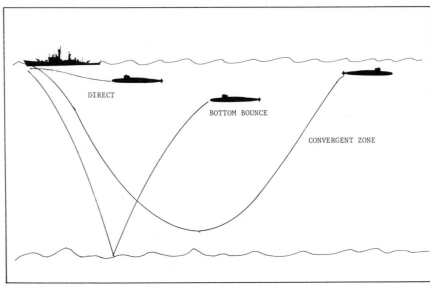

Figure 9 Typical multiple underwater sound propagation paths

Bibliography

Albers, V O *Underwater Acoustics Handbook* II The Pennsylvania State University Press, University Park, Pa, 1965

Albers, V O *The World of Sound*, A B Barnes & Co, Cranbury, NJ, 1970

Clay, C S and H Medwin *Acoustical Oceanography Principles and Applications* Wiley-Interscience, New York, 1977

Cohen, P *The Realm of the Submarine* The MacMillan Co, London, 1969

Stephens, R W B, (Ed) *Underwater Acoustics* Wiley-Interscience, London, 1970

Tucker, D G and B K Gazey *Applied Underwater Acoustics* Pergamon Press, Oxford, 1966

Urick, R J *Principles of Underwater Sound for Engineers* McGraw-Hill Book Co, New York, 1967

Anti-submarine sealions

● **by Richard Compton-Hall**

EVERY KIND OF DEVICE was considered at the onset of the 1914-1918 war to counter the devastating attacks of the new underwater enemy. In those days money was more plentiful and, for inventors, nothing lacked. As always, the simplest solutions proved best in the end, but some unusual answers to the U-boat problem were produced.

Among those anxious to offer their services were a number of psychic mediums who claimed they could sense the presence and position of enemy submarines off the English coast — and their efforts were by no means ridiculed

even if the results were a little unreliable. And then there was Sir Richard Paget who was said to have a very keen sense of pitch. To determine propeller frequencies, he was suspended by his legs over the side of a boat while a submarine circled him. After a suitable period submerged, and before he actually drowned, he was hauled up humming the notes he had heard

whereupon, safely back in the boat, he related them to the standard G-sharp which he obtained by tapping his cranium. This was helpful of Sir Richard but his efforts in the battle paled beside those of his colleagues at the Board of Invention and Research who conducted their business more comfortably at the optimistically named Victory House in Cockspur Street, London SW. The BIR was, of course, the forerunner of various Research and Development organisations that have since proliferated.

The gentlemen of the Board, which had been assembled at the instigation (not surprisingly) of Winston Churchill, then First Lord of the Admiralty, were directly responsible to the redoubtable Admiral Jackie Fisher, the First Sea Lord. They deserve a special place in history if only because they put in train through their Section II sub-committee some experiments with sealions to determine whether these animals could detect and trap submarines.

Backed as it was by the two most vigorous characters in naval history, the Board enjoyed a great deal of power and tended to give itself airs. On January 9, 1917, for instance, the Secretary pointed out aggrievedly in a docket that certain experiments proposed by the Admiralty had not been passed through the office of the BIR; but a certain Mr Threlfall sitting in Whitehall urged that, while the BIR had no doubt been very improperly treated, it was inexpedient to make formal objection, provided they were satisfied that the experiments were in competent hands.

All this was Civil Service play and counterplay — the usual overture to R & D at any time: much enjoyed by all concerned while the real action was at sea. Whether 'competent' hands was the right description is a matter of doubt but extensive trials of all sorts were conducted under the auspices of the BIR through the various Admiralty departments concerned. By May, 1917 sealions were figuring prominently amongst them, as the following (abbreviated) letter shows:

ADMIRALTY
May 17th 1917

Sir

I am commanded by My Lords Commissioners of the Admiralty to acquaint you that they have approved of a series of trials being carried out in the Solent in regard to the capabilities of Sealions in tracking submarines.

2 Rear Admiral B A Allenby (Retired) is in charge of these trials, and Their Lordships desire that you will place a submarine at his disposal for the trials and furnish him with all necessary facilities for this purpose.

3 Rear Admiral Allenby's requirements for the trials are as follows:

A stable or shed with water laid on, salt for choice.

A **suitable** *launch with small boat in tow, which launch could carry a cage*

with two animals. The launch should be as noiseless as possible. A suitable cage would require to be built, with a sloping gangway to be fitted for the animals to climb on board, unless the launch has a low gunwhale (3 feet).

A submarine of any class would suffice to train the animals. Preliminary trials at anchor on the surface, later submerged. There are no data to enable a definite opinion to be expressed as to how long the training with submarines would continue, but a decision might be arrived at, one way or another, in about a fortnight provided weather conditions were favourable.

4 You are requested to report to the Admiralty by telegraph when this trial will be ready to commence, observing that the

sealions will not be ready before 25th instant.

Admiral Superintendent
Flag Captain, Blockhouse

Signed   S C Colville, Admiral

Copy to each.

Dr E J Allen, the Director of the Marine Biological Laboratory at Plymouth, was the physicist appointed as the Board's representative and he immediately put himself in correspondence with the self-styled Captain Woodward, a well known trainer of performing sealions who was said at this time to be investigating the power of these animals to hear sounds in water.

... sealions undoubtedly had better facilities ...

Woodward claimed to have established already that 'they could hear quite weak sounds, such as the tinkle of a bell that is put on dog's collars, at speeds up to nine knots and they could tell the direction'.

Dr Allen studied the structure of the animal's ears and set himself to compare the listening ability of a sealion with that of a hydrophone. A good deal of experimental work was continuing with hydrophones at this time: but those developed so far, notably by a Commander Ryan, were too highly selective and recorded mainly their own characteristic frequencies which was not much help to the listeners. Sealions undoubtedly had better faculties.

It is clear that the renowned Captain Woodward realised from the start that he was on to a good thing and he was only too glad to supply sealions 'which were available in very large numbers' to the Admiralty. The trials were promptly put in hand and progressed at commendable speed. Ever helpful, Sir Richard Paget of the G-sharp cranium devised a muzzle made of wire with a small trap-door in front through which the animal could be fed. This prevented any sealion so equipped from catching fish and thereby being distracted from its duty.

Several animals were chosen for the experiment, foremost amongst them being Millicent, Billiken, Queenie and Dorande. The last named was getting on in years, dim-sighted and a little hard of hearing but his short-sightedness made him less prone to pursue fish so he was able to work unmuzzled. He was, in fact, so nearly blind that there was some difficulty in teaching him to jump accurately onto the boat from which the trials were directed. But with clearly spoken directions he soon managed quite well. He was the most reliable worker in the team and was quite happy to tow a large cigar-shaped float so that his course could be followed by eye from above.

The animals were encouraged to chase the target submarine by rewarding them with herrings but on one occasion these were bad: the failure of Billiken one day, following a hot spell, was attributed to this. He was off colour and disinclined to chase submarines for quite a while thereafter.

The conclusions following the trials were vague but the Board thought that 'the sounds made by a submarine when at rest or moving slowly are of very feeble intensity and not easily heard by the animals'. (Modern sonar R & D reports say something very similar although they do not put it so succinctly). Nor was a sealion's normal sustained speed (about five knots) great enough to overtake a submarine while 'passing vessels, as well as fish, proved a serious obstacle to success.'

Such was the awe in which the Board of Invention and Research was held that it took 14 years before the Admiralty ventured to ask how the trials had progressed. It was not, in fact, until 1931 (by which time the Board had long dispersed) that Their Lordships enquired from Rear Admiral Submarines whether any reports and photographs were readily available about the matter at the Submarine Headquarters. They were not.

Nor, sadly, is there any record of how Millicent, Billiken, Queenie and the dedicated deaf Dorande spent their declining years. It can only be hoped that Captain Woodward maintained them in the comfort to which they had become accustomed in the navy.

Sub-harpoon

TORPEDOES LIKE Tigerfish travel fast and far; but no wholly underwater weapon can compare with a missile for speed and range. Its qualities are more and more important for a submarine attacking a surface ship, especially for a nuclear submarine defending a task force or a convoy when speed is a vital factor. The enemy warships, themselves almost certainly armed with long-range missiles, cannot be allowed to come within striking range and there may well be no time to conduct the relatively long approach necessary to carry out a torpedo attack.

Even 20 years ago, before the Soviet fleet was anything like as well armed as it is today, it was clear that attack-class

● The editor examines British usage underwater of tactical missiles to replace guns

nuclear submarines (SSNs) were going to need tactical missiles to supplement torpedoes in order to deal effectively with the surface threat.

Meanwhile, something was needed to supersede a submarine's surface and anti-aircraft guns which were obviously outdated by ever increasing anti-submarine air cover. In particular, there was an urgent requirement to find a weapon that would knock down a helicopter; helicopters with dunking sonar and homing weapons had become the submariner's most difficult enemies to deal with by the 1960's.

As an interim solution, and as an inexpensive way of joining the missile-club initially, HMS Aeneas was equipped in 1970 with a battery of six Blowpipe anti-aircraft missiles normally used by the Army as man-portable weapons. The missiles were fitted on top of what had been the periscopic radar mast and they could be fired from periscope depth. The system, designated SLAM (Submarine-launched air-missile system), worked well enough but submariners felt it was something of a last-

ditch affair, not much more effective, perhaps, than physically ramming a dunked sonar ball — something accomplished in a near-court-martial situation by the Commanding Officer of *HMS Springer* in 1957. So *HMS Aeneas* became the first and possibly the last SSG in the RN: she finally paid off in 1972 when it was found that somebody had painted *SS Gillette* on her stern — a cynical forecast of the fate which awaited her.

It was not until May, 1971 that McDonnell Douglas Astronautics were awarded a 66 million dollar contract for developing the Surface-to-Surface Missile (SSM) which was to become first the ship-launched and then the submarine-launched missile named *Harpoon*. The main contract followed in July, 1973 and development was rapid. By 1975 some 30 prototype weapons had been launched, three of them from submarines.

Meanwhile, Britain had started to produce an Under-Sea Guided Weapon (USGW) unilaterally to rival the Soviet SS-N-7 Siren missiles carried by *Charlie* and *Papa*-class submarines which were supposed to have a submerged launch capability. The new USGW was to be called Sub-Martel and was largely based on the French Martel missile. However, collaboration with France was abandoned and the project was cancelled altogether in 1975 in favour of buying Harpoon from the USA.

Harpoon, as a standard sea-skimming missile maintained at the desired height by a radar altimeter and propelled at a high subsonic speed by a turbojet engine with ranges of 50 miles plus, was remarkably successful almost from the start. Its later developments are

Helicopter dunking-sonar ball about to be (deliberately) rammed and snagged with the starboard forward hydroplane. Seen through the periscope by the perpetrator (the author) commanding HMS Springer in 1957. At the time this seemed to be the only practical way of dealing with a menacing helicopter — and it worked! On the right is the suprised and infuriated helicopter pilot realising that his sonar ball has been written off

The Royal Navy's first SSG, HMS Aeneas,
pictured left before paying off in 1972

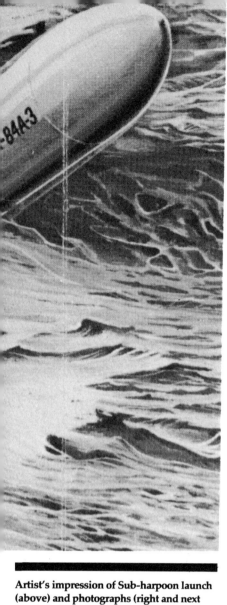

Artist's impression of Sub-harpoon launch (above) and photographs (right and next page). Below is a salvo of two Sub-harpoon missiles launched from HMS Courageous while submerged

highly classified but the missile's original homing system was an active radar seeker which searched, locked-on and finally commanded an abrupt pull-up and swoop down on the target from above. The heavy warhead was designed primarily to penetrate the target but was equipped both with proximity and impact delayed fuses.

The missile was well proven before being adapted for submarine use. With a length of 4.58 metres and a diameter of 343mm, there was no problem in loading it into standrd 21-inch (533mm) torpedo tubes.

The Royal Navy Sub-harpoon (RNSH) is contained in a capsule which is ejected from a submarine's torpedo tube just like a torpedo. When the missile clears the tube its control fins deploy and the capsule glides to the surface. On sensing the broach the nosecap and tail of the capsule is blown off and the missile slides out using a booster motor. After about three seconds the missile's main engine starts, the booster falls away and the missile ascends to its pre-programmed flight-level at which height the mid-course guidance systems steers it towards its target until the terminal homing system takes over.

Sub-harpoon can be launched in practically any sea conditions and from tactically convenient depths. At first there were understandable doubts about the capsule method of ejection with regard to the missile subsequently taking up its assigned flight paths but trials have been extremely successful — far more successful, in fact, than ordinary torpedo trials are apt to be.

Operating out of San Diego *HMS Courageous* fired 15 RN Sub-harpoon missiles between July 1981 and February, 1982 and achieved 100 per cent success. In addition to the missiles themselves, 81 verification rounds — inert missiles — were launched as part of the RN's assessment of the total system. By any standards, the results were astonishingly good. The new system will eventually be fitted in all British nuclear Attack-class submarines — the *Valiant*, *Swiftsure* and *Trafalgar* classes. At long last, submarines have a weapon which is compatible with their long-range sonar detection and classification ability: and there is every reason to believe that Sub-harpoon would be extremely effective in war.

Underwater doctoring 1914-19

Very few submarine officers knew how to apply an antiseptic dressing properly and it was common practice for the crew to help themselves to articles in the chest indiscriminately, thereby soiling rolls of cotton wool, cyanide gauze and bandages. Scissors were frequently used for purposes for which they were not designed and in one boat the crew habitually consumed soda-mint tablets as sweetmeats.
Surgeon Commander A D Cowburn, RNVR, Depot ship *HMS Ambrose*

I do not think that five submarine sailors in 100 clean their teeth at sea. Their teeth are usually in an unsanitary condition and, due partly to this and partly to constipation, their breath is normally bad at sea. I think the constipation of ratings is due to their own carelessness and ignorance, and it is difficult for officers to deal with this as the men do not willingly report their condition.
Commander J G Brown, DSO, RN, Commanding Officer *K12*.

● From manuscript reports from submarine commanding officers and staff medical officers, made to Rear Admiral Submarines in October 1919

The chief handicap to the efficiency of the submarine seaman is his tendency to constipation induced by over-eating, lack of exercise and inadequacy of conveniences. Some boats had no WC at all. Relief was generally discouraged until the boat came to the surface at night and I have heard of cases where men went without relief for four or five days. Personally I made a man take a pill every two days unless I was assured he had no need of it.
Lieutenant Commander G P Thomson OBE, Commanding Officer *E35*

Excluding the various forms of gas poisoning, I have seen no condition peculiar to the submarine service.
Surgeon Commander C R Rickard, Depot Ship *HMS Maidstone*

The practice of using the right eye only at the periscope is very common. I cannot see how it can be done away with entirely but efforts should be made individually to use both eyes equally.
Commander C S Benning, DSO HMS *Adamant*

I myself suffered from a form of this disease (Pyorrhea) known as 'French mouth' and a dental specialist blamed it on tinned food. This view was sufficiently well looked on by the Admiralty to make them refund me a very large bill for dental treatment.
Lieutenant Commander G P Thomas OBE, Commanding Officer *E35*

Underwater doctoring today, in nuclear submarines, is mainly concerned with atmosphere control and nuclear monitoring. Here LMA G T D Olsen is placing a radioactive sample in the counting chamber

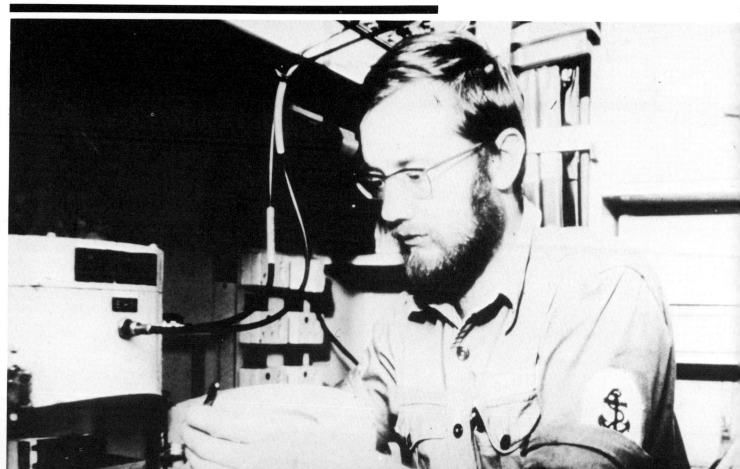

Fast turbine- driven non-nuclea

● by Lieutenant Commander Mike Wilson RN (Retired) who commanded three submarines during his service career, amongst them the HTP-propelled HMS Explorer 1961-1962. He is now the Submarine Historian at the Naval Historical Branch of the Ministry of Defence, Earls Court

DURING THE 1939-45 war, the Germans, and after the war the British and to a limited extend the Americans and Russians, experimented with turbine-driven submarines powered by the chemical products of the breakdown of a highly concentrated solution of hydrogen peroxide. This solution was variously known as perhydrol, ingolin or high test peroxide (HTP). The aim was to give the submarine a capability of a very high speed for a limited period, either to gain an attacking position or to escape once the boat had been detected. The advent of the nuclear-powered submarine rendered the project obsolete, and the system never became fully operational in any navy. Nevertheless, the story of the development of this novel propulsion system, and of what was achieved in the quarter-century 1939 to 1964 is worthy of record.

Even in the early days of the war the German naval staff were interested in the problem of producing a 'true submarine', one that had the ability to travel at reasonable under-water speeds and needing either no time on the surface or a bare minimum. This became more and more important as allied air power made it increasingly unsafe for the U-boat to remain on the surface. One answer, provided originally by the Dutch navy, was to fit schnorchel tubes to all submarines. This was done not only to new construction but also retrospectively to existing boats as they returned from patrol; the first to be fitted being the *U264* in September, 1943.

Further improvement required a new design of U-boat, with a more streamlined hull shape and an increased battery capacity. This was the Type XXI and its smaller sister, the Type XXIII. The allies must count themselves lucky that the advent of these two new types was delayed both by production difficulties and the diversification of effort onto other designs. The delay was crucial, for the war was over before they could be deployed operationally in sufficient numbers to have affected the battle, but their success in the few cases where these boats were able to carry out operational patrols underlines the problems that would have confronted the Allies had they come to fruition.

Another promising development, the subject of this story, lay in the turbine designed by Professor Helmuth Walter and which bears his name. Laboratory experiments were successfully conducted in 1939, and in April 1940 a specially designed submarine, the *V80* (V: *Versuchsboote*, Research ship; 80 = 80 tonnes) of only 73 tons (surface)/76 tons (dived) was launched to take the system to sea for trials. She had no armament and had a civilian rather than a naval crew.

Briefly, the system relied on the breakdown of a high concentration of hydrogen peroxide in a catalyst chamber to form oxygen and steam. The initial trials used only these products of decomposition to power the turbine and to avoid making these trials over-complicated the combustion of a fuel was not added to the process until a later date.

Manufacture and storage of the

The experimental German V80 in about 1940 with civilian crew in soft hats. The boat was later modified to give a forecasing and clipper bow for better sea-keeping

ubmarines

U-1407, scuttled May 2, 1945 at Cuxhaven, salvaged by the British and towed to Barrow for refit before becoming HMS Meteorite. The boat is shown here after being raised

hydrogen peroxide fuel was a problem in itself. Dr Walter used it at an 80% concentration, far removed from the mild disinfectant or hair bleach that may be bought over the counter at a chemist's shops. In this form it is highly volatile, is easily decomposed, often in a violent fashion, and will react with most materials normally used as storage containers.

Trials with the V80 were conducted throughout 1941 and speeds of 26 knots were recorded. Towards the end of 1942 further trials were undertaken mainly to measure performance as well as to test

ancillary equipment such as the automatic depth and steering equipment. The major tests were then concluded and there remained only three exhibition runs in 1943. The boat remained at Hela until March 29, 1945, when it was towed into Danzig Bay and destroyed with three depth charges to prevent capture by the advancing Russians. Certain parts were evacuated to Keil, including the special reduction gearing, where they were subsequently captured when the British Army entered the port in May 1945, and from there taken to the Vickers Armstrong

shipyard at Barrow-in-Furness.

After the V80 had begun trials the next stage was a large boat, the V300, intended to be a seagoing prototype. The final design of September, 1941 was of 610 tons surface displacement (655 tons dived); she was 171 feet long and fitted with two Walter turbines. With 98 tons of perhydrol it was hoped to achieve a range of 205 miles at 19 knots. Conventional diesel-electric drive was included in the design for normal manoeuvres. Two torpedo tubes, forward, would complete the design. As a naval crew was subsequently

115

proposed for the trials with this submarine the boat was later given the number *U791*, but in the event it was an academic change since in the summer of 1942 construction work was stopped because with the increased size the designed top speed was not as high as that of a destroyer in medium seas and running against the sea. This principle was considered of prime importance by Dr Walter. Nevertheless it was felt that the project was a success. Indeed on 22 December 1942 Admiral Raeder in a personal report to Hitler advised that a decision could then be taken on the mass production of 24 small boats and the commissioning of larger experimental boats for further trials. Despite this report and the backing of Admiral Doenitz there was a lack of urgency in giving the design full priority.

The next series of U-boats to be powered by the Walter turbine, by then incorporating combustion of oil fuel in the process, were the four submarines *U792 - 795* of the Type XVIIA (or Wa 201/WK 202); two built by Blohm and Voss, the other two by Germania Werft at Kiel. They were coastal submarines of 236/259 tons carrying two torpedo tubes. Like all submarines of the time the hull shape was long and thin with a length/breadth ratio of about 10:1, but even so it was hoped that the two turbines geared to drive one shaft would be able to produce a top speed in excess of 25 knots.

The complement was 12. Construction started in December 1942 and the first two boats arrived at Hela for trials in November 1943, the others in May 1944. Because of production difficulties the last two boats, *U793* and *U795*, were fitted with only one turbine each. These trials were completed, on the whole, satisfactorily; although because of slight design differences the Blohm and Voss boats were not only about two knots faster but also suffered less defects from their Keil sisters. The four boats were never operational and were scuttled in May 1945.

It was originally intended to follow up the four Type XVIIA submarines with a series of 196 operational boats of the Type XVIIB. By the time it was possible to order these boats priority had been given to the more promising types XXI and XXIII and the number of Walter turbine boats was reduced to 24, Blohm and Voss and Germania Werft each supplying 12. They were to have been powered by two turbines coupled to a single shaft but continued delays in the production of the turbine led to a further redesign and the five boats built or building at the war's end had only one. Production of perhydrol towards the end of the war also caused worries for

the German navy since their allocation was constantly being reduced due to Luftwaffe claims for a bigger share of the limited amount available for their V weapons. In addition to the one turbine, which gave a theoretical best speed of 21½ knots, the boats were fitted with normal diesel/electric drive and armed with two torpedoes. Three boats, *U1405, 1406* and *1407* had been completed by the war's end, and were then scuttled by their German crews.

At least two other Types, XVIII and XXVI, were planned but not put into production. The Type XVIII with six torpedo tubes was to be a boat of about 1,800 tons equipped with two turbines and based on the design of the Type XXI fast electric boat. The Type XXVI was again slightly smaller at 1,000 to 1,200 tons and with one turbine. It was a novel design in that it had four forward torpedo tubes and six amidships at the sides of the hull pointing aft. No reload torpedoes were incorporated in the design.

The system operated basically on a turbine activated by the decomposition of a high concentration of hydrogen peroxide; in the initial trials, as stated earlier, the resultant gases were at a sufficiently high pressure and temperature to drive the turbine on their own. The breakdown of the peroxide occurred in the catalyst chamber where it passed over the catalyst and resulted in steam and oxygen at more than 1700°F. These gases were then led away to a combustion chamber where oil fuel was injected and ignited. Water was also sprayed in with the combustion products, increasing the volume of the gas and bringing the temperature down to 986°F. The gas was then passed into the turbine and from there into the

HMS Explorer during surface speed trials in April 1957, and shown right some two months before being accepted into service in May 1956

condenser. The condenser acted to separate the water from the cooled gas and extract the remaining gases, mostly carbon dioxide, for discharge overboard where they were dissolved in the sea water.

Since early 1943 allied intelligence had included reports of a fast U-boat being developed by the Germans, named 'Walterboote' after the designer and with reputed speeds of up to 30 knots submerged. The first positive evidence of their existence was found at the Blohm and Voss shipyard at Hamburg which was entered on May 3, 1945 by personnel of 30 Assault Unit, a Royal Marine Commando Unit formed to capture material of an operational nature for intelligence purposes. Here, two U-boats, U1408 and U1410, were found lying heavily damaged on the jetty. A bomb had fallen between them while completing on the slips and they had been lifted out of the way and all work had been suspended. Despite the damage and the removal of certain parts thre was enough left for the examining technical officers to know that these were the first examples of the new Walter U-boat to be seen by the Allies. On May 4 another section of 30 Assault Unit RM made a rapid advance into Kiel, took over the Walterwerke, which was largely undamaged, and captured Dr Walter and his staff. Interrogations were carried out by both British and US officers and the whole story of the Walter submarines, and that of his many other projects, came to light. Later all documents were removed for study; scrap weapons and storage tanks were destroyed and the chemicals removed.

Two submarines were salvaged, the U1407 and 1406; the former was taken to the Vickers Armstrong shipyard at Barrow while the latter was shipped to the USA.

Not much is known of the extent to which the US authorities continued with Dr Walter's system. With the advent of the nuclear submarine Nautilus in 1952 it would seem unlikely that further development was prolonged. The U1406 herself was scrapped in May, 1948. Nevertheless the midget submarine X1, designed and built by the Fairchild Engine and Airplane Corporation of Long Island, was launched on September 7, 1955 and completed the following month. She was 50 feet long and had a standard surface displacement of 29 tons. There was no armament. A small scale HTP system was available for dived operations. In early 1958 a severe explosion broke the hull into three sections, but the boat was salvaged, refitted in Philadelphia Navy Yard, and brought back into commission in December, 1960 for further experimental work. Whether or not at this stage of nuclear development the HTP plant was retained is not known. What is even more interesting is that the 1953-54 edition of Jane's Fighting Ships lists a projected HTP boat of some 2,200 tons to have been built at Portsmouth Navy Yard. That the projected design was soon dropped is reflected by its absence from the following edition.

The Russians also carried out some experiments with this form of propulsion after the war. It can be assumed that they acquired some

know-how from the Germans in their zone of occupation and from captured equipment, although there were no Type XVII's among the ten U-boats alocated to them after the German surrender. When the Americans occupied a huge underground factory near Blankenberg in the Harz mountains they found a full scale wooden mock-up for the U4501, the first Type XXVI boat. This was left when the area was later handed over to the Red Army.

There is reason to believe that the Russians did fit Walter turbines in the early boats of both the Zulu and Quebec classes of submarines in the early 1950's. Both classes had three shafts; in the case of the Zulus the turbines were fitted on the outer two shafts, while the submarines of the Quebec class had one turbine only on the centre shaft. It is understood that this arrangement could not have been found satisfactory and that these boats were all retrofitted with conventional diesel-electric drive on all shafts, as were subsequent boats of the classes.

Now the story returns to Barrow on the north west coast of England where the U1407 had been taken in the autumn of 1945. While experts investigated the Walter power plant the rest of the boat was refitted and partially re-equipped. It was the Admiralty's intention to conduct trials with the idea of introducing its method of propulsion to give the Royal Navy's new submarines a high speed capability.

As the boat was to be used initially purely for trials, and possibly later only for A/S training, the torpedo tubes were

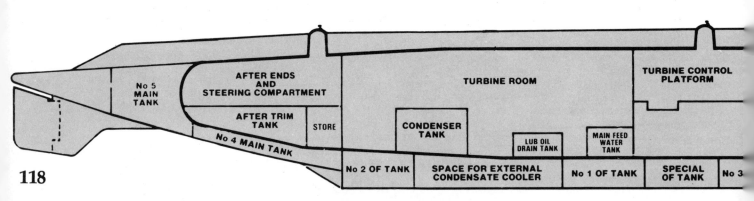

removed during the refit and hull openings blanked off. Again, it was considered that the schnorchel would not be required in these circumstances and it, too, was removed. Other major work involved changing the battery ventilation system to bring it into line with British practice, the fitting of escape equipment and an additional air compressor while removing the high pressure air system to operate the main vents. All the electrical gear had to be completely refitted following her scuttling at the end of the war. Even so, all this work was completed ahead of that on the turbine plant so it was decided to start trials of the handling of the boat as a 'conventional' submarine and to give her crew of four officers and 12 ratings an oppportunity to become fully acquainted with her characteristics.

In June, 1947 the *U1407* became *HMS Meteorite*. In February of that year the Commanding Officer, Lieutenant J S Launders RN, applied for permission to continue to use the badge of the *U1407* painted on the front of the bridge. The badge, consisting of a shark and a gallows angled against a helmsman's wheel, was considered by Launders to be apt for the boat in view of the punishments meted out at the War Crimes' trials. The symbolism was regarded as the cynical view of the original German CO: the wheel offered a Hobson's choice between the crew becoming food for the sharks if the boat was handled with the requisite daring necessary for results, or disgrace if caution were employed. The Admiralty did not agree with this proposal and with the change of name a more

The launch of HM Submarine Torpedo Boat number 1

'It is understood that no ceremony will take place at the forthcoming launch of the first British submarine at Barrow-in-Furness. The Admiralty regard these boats as wholly in the nature of an experiment, and, like all other experiments conducted from time to time, this one will be carried out with every privacy.'

Naval and Military Record October 3, 1901

heraldically correct badge was authorised displaying a golden meteor on a wavy barred field of blue and white.

The initial trials were completed in the middle of March, 1948. It was considered that the boat was slow to respond at the low speeds used for the trials, but that she was stable and everything pointed towards a good response at high speed. The combustion plant underwent trials ashore in Barrow from July to September 1947 and after the rectification of a number of flaws the shore trials were completed in July, 1948. The plant was then refitted in the submarine. Surface trials were delayed by bad weather but were completed by October, 1948. Results were promising besides giving the crew considerable confidence in handling both plant and fuel. A speed of 14½ knots was obtained. One interesting phenomenon

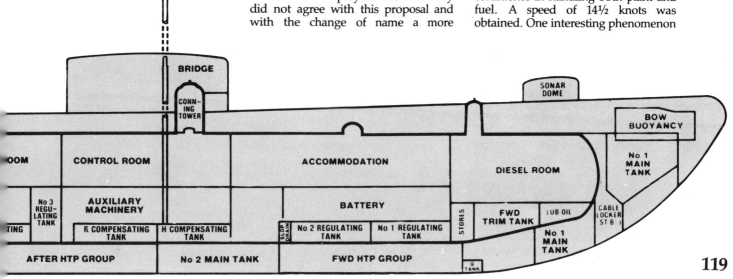

was noted. As the surface speed of the submarine increased the second bow wave moved aft along the comparatively short length of the submarine lifting up the stern, until at full speed it actually moved astern of the boat, whereupon the boat returned to an even keel. However, the cavity formed forward of the second bow wave was sufficient to slow down the boat, although when dived this would not occur and it was hoped to achieve an extra three knots speed. This was borne out in early 1949 when dived trials were successfully carried out.

The *Meteorite* (ex *U1407*) had completed her job and all was now set for the next, and final, stage of this interesting project. The *Meteorite* herself was paid off on July 8, 1949 and was handed over to the British Iron and Steel Corporation for scrap later that year.

It is now necessary to revert to 1945 when a submarine to be propelled by HTP machinery was included in the new construction programme with a second such boat included in the 1947/48 programme. Nevertheless no work was started and the results of the *Meteorite* trials were awaited. The Admiralty remained enthusiastic for in the 1949/50 programme it was stated that it was planned to build 14 new submarines by 1955 to replace the 'S' Class and indicated that six of these boats would be fitted with HTP propulsion. However doubts began to creep in, not the least

being the fear that the supply of HTP would be insufficient to maintain this number of boats in an operational state. With the completion of the *Meteorite* trials it was decided to go ahead with the two boats already programmed and one was eventually laid down on July 20, 1951 and the second on February 13 the following year. The two submarines completed as *HMS Explorer* and *Excalibur* in November, 1956 and March 1958 respectively. By comparison with the *Meteorite* (and the German Type XVIIB's) they were larger boats being of 1,100 tons surface displacement, 1,200 tons dived. They had a length of 225½ ft overall (which compared to *Meteorite's* 136¾ ft) were 15ft 9½ins in beam and had a draught of 17ft 9ins. There was only one periscope, no torpedo tubes and no radar. An unusual feature was the Paxman diesel engine which was fitted forward in what would normally have been the torpedo reload compartment. This engine recharged the batteries and was used for the normal diesel electric drive when on passage on the surface. An economical speed of about six knots could be achieved depending on weather and tide! Accommodation was limited although it was unnecessary to take the full crew to sea. Accordingly each submarine was allocated a small tender to act as a living ship when the submarines were detached for exercises, and to carry the bulkier items of stores and spare gear. An additional role was that of safety vessel for the submarine when operating alone, in view of the submarine's low profile which made then a poor radar or visual target and also as the submarines themselves were without radar. The ships allocated for this role were two small wartime constructed minelayers; *HMS Miner VIII* (later renamed *HMS Mindful*) with the *Explorer*, and *HMS Miner I* (renamed *HMS Minstrel*) with the *Excalibur*.

One other ship comes into the story — the Royal Fleet Auxiliary *Spabeck*. Built during the war for harbour duties as a water carrier to the fleet she was converted to act as a mobile HTP depot for the two submarines. For this purpose she was fitted with ten tanks which enabled her to take 111 tons of the fuel from the main depot at Faslane to wherever either of the submarines was operating. For safety's sake it was decided to limit fuelling operations to

daylight hours only, which was done in harbour and not underway. Additionally she was able to carry more than 17 tons of special sulphur-free AVCAT (aviation jet fuel) injected into the combustion chamber during the turbine propulsion cycle.

During the first-class trials the *Explorer* exceeded 26½ knots, but neither submarine was satisfactory in service. Despite all the development work by the Germans and by Vickers they were plagued with minor defects in the HTP system, not the least being salt water contamination of the HTP due to leaks in the plastic bags. What could they achieve? At full speed the two boats had a reputed endurance of nearly three hours during which time they used nearly 100 tons of HTP. By reducing the throughput to the combustion chamber or by using only one of the two turbines endurance could be increased considerably. At slow speed on one turbine, about 12 knots, there was an endurance of about 15 hours, although in practice this long endurance was seldom employed because of the physical limitations on the crew. Strangely, they were poor sonar targets, at least with active sonar.

Each submarine did two commissions with a refit in between before paying off into reserve and subsequently being sold for scrap; the *Explorer* decommissioned in June, 1962 and the *Excalibur* at the end of 1963. They came too late into a submarine world which in the post war years increasingly turned its eyes and thoughts to ideas of nuclear propulsion. One can but speculate on the effect that such boats would have had on the Battle of the Atlantic, and wonder, too, how their delicate 'spurt machinery' would have stood up to the realities of depth charging.

One further aspect deserves mention; the development of a fast submarine torpedo. An ordinary British Mk 8 torpedo was taken and modified to run on the break-down products of HTP. Under its new designation of Mk 12, or Fancy, it was issued to the submarine depot ship *HMS Maidstone* at Portland in the summer of 1955 for trials. One June morning a torpedo in *HMS Sidon*, having been loaded into the tube for test firing, blew up while the submarine was still alongside. She sank with the loss of 13 lives. Later another

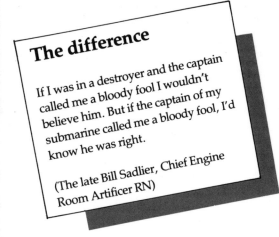

The difference

If I was in a destroyer and the captain called me a bloody fool I wouldn't believe him. But if the captain of my submarine called me a bloody fool, I'd know he was right.

(The late Bill Sadlier, Chief Engine Room Artificer RN)

torpedo exploded on the test range at Arrochar in Scotland and the torpedo was withdrawn.

Ironically the Swedes developed successfully the Tp 61 high speed torpedo using the details of the Mk 12 and results of the *Sidon* enquiry. It had been our mistake to develop a torpedo using such a highly volatile fuel by modifying an existing weapon rather than starting anew using only materials which were not affected by the HTP.

Was it all worth while? In retrospect perhaps not, but as with earlier experiments to produce a fast submarine, like the RN's steam driven 'K' class, it is an era of development that must be remembered.

Down from the hills

... and distant but unmistakeable skirl of the pipes

IT WAS ONE of those glassy calm evenings in the Minches. The exercises for the day had finished early and the submarine was able to anchor in the middle of a small bay well before sunset. There was a faint creaking of winches from the tiny fishing village at the head of the harbour.

All was peaceful. It may well have been a hundred years since any other warship had disturbed the silence with the heavy splash of iron cable. It seemed a sin to start the noisy diesels and recharge the batteries. Deliberately I delayed giving the order.

Sensing, I suppose, that something was wrong with the routine, our aged, and very Scottish, Chief Stoker climbed ponderously up to the bridge. I greeted him and pointed out the beauties of the scene surrounding us, the deep blues and greens, the scent of pine with just a touch of herring in it, the . . . and at that moment there drifted across the still waters the faint, and distant but unmistakeable skirl of the Pipes. It put, so to speak, the finishing touch to a picture already unbearably evocative.

I turned to the Chief Stoker and asked him softly what the Highland music meant. He spat accurately over the side. 'Sirr,' he said, rolling every 'r' in range, 'young Robbie at the lighthouse there will have told them we were coming'. He spat again. 'Och, the noo they're piping the whoorres down from the hills . . .'

The monstrous midgets

● by Richard Compton-Hall

TAKING COMMAND of a midget submarine in the Royal Navy was rather like being given a toy train set for Christmas. Everything was in miniature; but the controls and the machinery were perfectly recognisable to a submariner coming from bigger boats.

Britain, Italy, Germany and Japan all built midgets of one kind or another which saw service in World War II and the Royal Navy maintained a small X-craft Unit until 1957. Thereafter, warlike mini-submersibles were abandoned and development was concentrated in the commercial field where techniques learned during the war have been developed and greatly improved, so far as diving capabilities and machinery are concerned, for deep underwater survey, engineering work and salvage. Wartime potential has largely been forgotten except, possibly, by the Soviet Navy who acquired advanced German and Japanese craft in 1945 and doubtless took careful note of their capabilities. In fact there was a suggestion recently that one of the mystery submarines hunted and almost caught in Swedish territorial waters could have been an amphibious midget: tank-like tracks were reputedly found on the sea-bed but who the vehicle belonged to can only be guessed.

If the Russians have developed midgets they have kept very quiet about them. Midget submarines have always been high on the secret list and trials, as well as actual operations, can be conducted secretively without too much difficulty. That is why so little is known or remembered today about those mini-monsters of World War II. It may be that small navies in particular, Israel's for example, are reconsidering their employment; for the years between 1940 and 1945 proved midgets to be immensely powerful and extremely economical both in terms of cost and personnel — but only when the men that manned them were thoroughly trained and properly employed on well-planned operations.

The Italians showed the way with their human torpedoes — *Maiale* or 'Pigs' — which sank a number of merchant ships and seriously damaged *HMS Queen Elizabeth* and *HMS Valiant* in Alexandria Harbour, reversing at a stroke the naval balance of power in the Mediterranean at the end of 1941. These craft, like the British chariots which

followed them, were simply slowed-down torpedoes driven by a mixture of air and oil with two operators, in shallow-water diving suits, sitting astride their craft one behind the other. Number One controlled the Pig with a type of joy stick and rudimentary trimming controls and Number Two assisted in fixing the large explosive charge, detached from the nose, to the underside of a target with wires or magnetic clamps.

Pigs and Chariots were potent and important units but unlike the British X-Craft, they were not really submarines. They had a limited endurance and could operate independently only for short periods in favourable conditions, although they penetrated defended harbours with alarming ease. But endurance was not the only factor. The Japanese had much less success than the other navies with mini-submersibles because most of them were suicidal in intent. It was one things for a Kamikaze pilot to dedicate

his life to the Emperor and crash his aircraft into an enemy warship; but it was quite another to maintain a suicide-craft's machinery at peak efficiency over a relatively long period — days or even weeks at sea on a parent submarine — and then navigate and manoeuvre, with the accuracy required of all submarine operations, with the virtual certainty of death ahead. In other navies midget operations were extremely hazardous but every effort was made to recover the crews after a mission: neither engineers nor seamen would have been at their most efficient in an end-game situation!

Bravery was not enough for midget operations. First-class seamanship and engineering skills were essential qualities; and those demanded rigorous training in depth — both senses. All submariners were — and still are — engineers to some extent; but midget submariners needed to know their craft intimately in every detail. There was no good shouting for help from Chief because there was no Engineer Officer;

and although a British X-Craft carried a competent Engine Room Artificer, he often doubled as a diver and was not necessarily available if machinery went wrong.

The Royal Navy's X-Craft were certainly the most interesting breed of midget both from an operational and engineering point of view. They were built, primarily, to deal with the giant battleship *Tirpitz* holed up in a Norwegian fjord where no other kind of vessel could reach her. The tiny submersibles had to be fully independent and they needed powerful weapons. The two requirements were well met in a craft about 50 feet long and looking remarkably like *HM Submarine No 1* launched far back in 1901 to the design of John Philip Holland.

The widely diverse tasks which X-Craft undertook after duly dealing with the *Tirpitz* in 1943 are well recorded: they included sea-bottom telephone cable-cutting; and two midgets actually

spearheaded the Normandy invasion by acting as beach markers for the amphibious tank landings. But little has been written about the outstandingly good and simple engineering principles that enabled them to achieve such extraordinary successes at so small a cost. Engineers may agree that the best type of machinery is usually the simplest; and everything in an X-Craft was as simple as could be. Handraulics were preferred to hydraulics; DC electrics were used throughout; the 42 hp engine had been proven thoroughly in London buses where it properly belonged; and the 30 hp electric motor was rugged to the point that it seemed capable of putting up with any amount of damp and dirt.

The battery consisted of 112 lead-acid cells, enabling the motor to be run with armatures in series at 220 volts, or in parallel at 110 volts with a 405 ampere/hour capacity at the five-hour discharge rate. A craft could make six and a half

HMS Stickleback (X-51) on the crane at Portland in 1956. The type of side-cargo fitted here is for carrying limpet mines. Two of the three antennae can be seen in this folded position: they were raised before coming up under a target to attach limpets, and below, looking forward over the helmsman's shoulder through the wet-and-dry compartment and 'heads' to the battery compartment. Main vent hand-levers are overhead

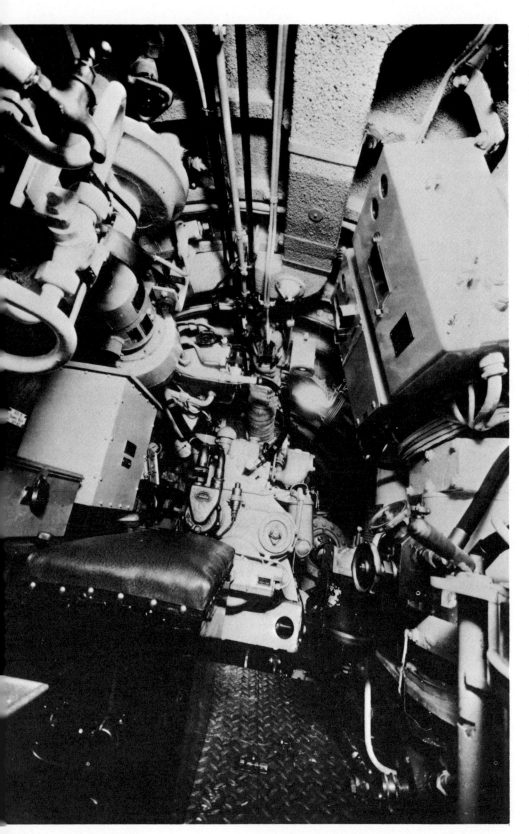

knots on the surface and about five knots submerged at top speed.

Two-ton Amatex 'side-cargoes' were slung, streamlined, on either side of the pressure hull and were released from inside the craft with a clockwork time-fuse mechanism. An X-Craft's range on the surface was 1,320 miles at four knots with a running battery charge or 1,860 miles if only floating the domestic load.

With a crew of four including the Captain the endurance was thus limited not by the propulsion but by human factors which, in theory anyway, could be stretched to an operation lasting between seven and ten days. Nonetheless, the operation against the Japanese cruiser *Takao*, which lasted for 52 hours, came close to the realistic limit for the crew and the strain of offensive operations, during which sleep was impossible, was well recognised even by the hardest hard-hearted Staff living in the comparative luxury of a Depot Ship! Each craft, therefore, had two crews: one undertook the long passage to the operational area during which a craft was towed by a parent submarine, both boats usually remaining submerged in daylight hours and the craft itself more

The engine-room of HMS Stickleback looking aft towards the Perkins diesel and shown right at Fort Blockhouse in 1956. The (passive) sonar dome is abaft the small periscope standard. Just forward of the standard is the so-called night periscope which could not be raised. The net-cutting periscope, manned by the electrical rating in the Battery compartment, is just abaft the bows. The Captain (Lt D J D Strang) is giving motor and wheel orders through the engine air-intake mast which also served (not very satisfactorily) as a voice-pipe

often remaining submerged throughout except for brief excursions to the surface every six hours to 'guff through', refreshing the air and charging the battery as necessary. When within about 50 miles of the target zone, the operational crew, hopefully fresh and rested, were ferried across in a rubber dinghy to relieve the passage crew who, after a long tow, were apt to be more than a little weary.

The operational crew, of course, were exposed to the greatest dangers but the passage crew were not without a few of these themselves. If the heavy tow-rope parted, for example, its weight could take the craft straight to the bottom, usually far beyond the maximum safe diving depth of 300 feet. The passage team worked hard. In northern waters work at least helped to keep away the cold — a damp, grey almost tangible variety that no kind of clothing could keep out. There were electrical installations to be checked; equipment to be tested; bilges to be dried; machinery to be greased and oiled; records to be written up; and the whole craft had to be kept scrupulously clean — a matter of particular pride.

Meanwhile meals, such as they were, had to be prepared. There was, needless to say, no galley. A carpenter's glue-pot in the control room served as a double boiler; and an electric kettle provided hot water. Although appetites quickly dwindled some attempt was made to cook regular meals for the first few days of a long tow. That is to say the first tins which came to hand out of the bilges were emptied into the glue-pot, heated and stirred into an unidentifiable pot mess. It was not an attractive repast but its memory remained until the next 'guff through'; the odour permeated the craft and condensation trickled drearily down the inside of the pressure hull. It was difficult to be truly thankful for food in these circumstances but one Engine Room Artificer, whose gratitude could only be admired (and he was seasick anyway), knelt to say an excessive grace before and after each meal. Midget submarine engineers were made of stern stuff!

There was, incidentally, a far more comfortable way of getting from point to point — by rail. If railway lines had been available to Kaa Fjord and Singapore, midget submariners would undoubt-

edly have bought tickets. Crews travelling around England with their craft in this way found railwaymen were a congenial crowd, quite willing to accede to eccentric whims and wishes. Trains were known to stop for the crews to shoot pheasants, refresh themselves at favourite hostelries en route and make whatever purchases were necessary to ensure their well-being. It was not always easy, however, to persuade railway police, when returning from one of these sorties to a marshalling yard in the middle of England, that a few innocent sailors were simply rejoining their warship on a railway siding.

In hostile waters, when the passage crew had paddled back to the towing submarine, the operational crew slipped the tow and settled themselves into the position they would occupy for the next two days or more. It was usual to stay deep for as long as possible so that an economical speed of two or three knots could be maintained without broaching. This quiet period while deep gave the crew a final opportunity to check and recheck every piece of equipment. Practically all the controls could be worked from the First Lieutenant's

position at the after end of the control room. All he lacked in equipment was enough hands and feet. He controlled the trim pump, main engine, battery charging, auxiliary electrics and hydroplanes. If the helmsman left his wheel — while helping the diver to dress for example — the First Lieutenant could also steer by clutching a secondary wheel on the hydroplane control. The trim was tender; a plate of stew and a cup of coffee passed from aft to forward could cause a bow-down angle. First Lieutenants came from a chosen race; no one-man band approached their performance.

The diver, too, had a difficult job. He had two main tasks. If limpet mines were selected for the operation rather than the huge explosive side-cargoes, he had to fix them with magnetic pads to the target's hull which was usually encrusted with weed and limpets that had to be scraped away. He also had to cut a way through any nets that barred the passage. He did this with a net-cutter that looked rather like an outsize tree-pruner: in cold and muddy water it was all too easy to substitute a finger for a strand of wire and scarcely notice the difference while the steel blade was

remorselessly doing its work. All this time the enemy was prone to drop random scare charges as a deterrent. It used to be explained patiently to divers that being scared was contrary to the Naval Discipline Act.

The diver left and re-entered the craft through a Wet and Dry lock which also housed the heads, a primitive, hazardous type of WC on which he sat while water was pumped up around him from an internal tank to avoid disturbing the trim. When it filled the tiny compartment the pump exerted its full pressure very suddenly on each and every part of the diver that was compressible, water itself unfortunately being incompressible and totally inelastic. The phenomenon was known, without much affection, as The Squeeze. Artificers who trained as X-Craft divers learned about hydraulic principles (if they had not paid attention at school) in a particularly hard way.

Attacks were carried out by the eyeball method. The Captain took the craft down to about 60 feet when some 300 yards short of the target which, of course, had to be moored alongside or at anchor. He then drove the craft on until the vast shape of the hull loomed

overhead, visible through an upper glass port close to the periscope amidships. The craft was then stopped by going astern on the screw and brought up to rest against special spring-loaded antennae like a fly on the ceiling if limpet mines were to be attached; or alternatively it was kept hovering or bottomed while the side-cargoes were released. With the fuses ticking away, the craft then thankfully turned around and made for the rendezvous with the parent submarine.

The enemy, naturally, had other ideas and did his best to make life difficult but losses were relatively light due, mainly, to thoroughly sound construction, strict adherence to basic engineering principles and extreme gallantry tempered by sound submarine practice.

Fourteen Victoria Crosses were awarded to British submariners in both World Wars: four of them, deservedly, went to X-Craft men and other awards included two Distinguished Service Medals and two Conspicuous Gallantry Medals to ERA's. Twenty-six men were killed in X-Craft but the cost to the enemy was incomparably heavy including a battleship and a cruiser disabled.

HMS Stickleback in floating dock at Portland, 1956. One of four similar X-craft launched 1954-55, Stickleback was bought by Sweden in 1958 and given back in 1976 when she was put on display with the Imperial War Museum's collection at Duxford

These extraordinary and versatile craft must seem extremely basic to the point of being crude today. But that was where their strength lay. Doubtless more sophisticated equipment could have been installed but the strength of an X-Craft lay in its omission.

The Royal Navy built four midgets of a new type in 1954-1955 — *Stickleback, Minnow, Shrimp* and *Sprat.* They carried one additional crew member bringing the total to five; and the equipment was supposedly an improvement on the wartime X and XE classes. But, frankly, the craft were little better and their handling characteristics worse. One notable addition was a W/T and voice radio together with a set of basic morse instructions which included an invaluable group, in effect, telling all other stations to keep quiet and listen carefully because the operator was inexperienced — which indeed he was. Its use brought all signal traffic on that frequency to a standstill and was unpopular!

Nor were midget submariners themselves popular in peace-time. Nobody outside the clan really understood what X-Craft could do or how they did it; and some of the exercises were decidedly risky outside a wartime situation. Then, too, X-Craft commanding officers had strange habits and were prone to conform to naval formalities in their own individual ways. A favourite trick, for example, was to trim a craft right down so that scarcely anything showed above the surface. While making his way down harbour the Captain would duly salute the vastly senior officers in command of surface ships he passed; but his habit of smartly marking time meanwhile gave an impression of walking on water that was by no means his of right.

All in all, it is not surprising that the British X-Craft Unit was soon disbanded. Some say that Flag Officer Submarines, on being invited to reduce the submarine fleet by four hulls in the interests of economy, craftily substituted the four midgets. But it is more likely that the gilded Staffs ashore simply did not like them!

Whatever the reason, there are no X-Craft in the Royal Navy today and the United Stated Navy only toyed briefly with the idea, quickly discarding the sole *X1* propelled by a frighteningly advanced high test peroxide engine.

It could well be argued that the lack of midget submarines in NATO navies is a serious omission — particularly if the Soviet Navy is employing them. Apart from the possible need for anti-submarine systems to combat the tiny craft, which are hard to detect by sonar, the training which X-Craft afforded young submarine officers was unique and exceptionally valuable. But above all else, X-Craft were, in today's language of economics, the most cost-effective type of submarine ever built.

It ought to be remembered, too, when considering a conceivable threat by the Soviet Union or from small nations and terrorist organisations, that a midget submarine is well suited to placing mines and nuclear, chemical or biological weapons in defended harbours and inshore areas where other vehicles might not be able to penetrate.

Amidst the complexity of the huge vessels going about their business under the water today, it may be that there is still a lesson to be learned from the superbly simple, cheap and nasty little X-Craft that contributed so much to the Royal Navy's success at sea during the last World War.

Bang on Bootle

IT WAS ONE of Bootle's bad days. It started at 0900 when Captain's defaulters were summoned to muster in the narrow passage forward of the submarine's control room. In fact it turned out that there was only one — Bootle well accustomed to these solitary ceremonies. The submarine was rolling horribly; and last night's refreshment, consumed in a particularly dark bar near the docks in the Vieux Port of Marseilles was taking its toll. Bootle wondered vaguely which of several bottles was responsible. A firm believer in sampling as many of the local products as possible, he had done unusually well on this occasion.

With a precision born of long practice

● by Richard Compton-Hall

Bootle took exactly the right amount of paces to the defaulter's table and removed his cap before the Coxswain had a chance to tell him to. This annoyed the Coxswain who proceeded, in a voice filled with menace, to make the formal introduction of the criminal to the judge. The judge — the Captain, that is — was painfully aware of Bootle's identity already but each time they faced each other across the table the Coxswain's bit about, 'Bootle, P/HX 96749 . . . ' etc had to be said all over again. Bootle always thought it rather rude of the Coxswain not to say who the Captain was as well.

Aunt Edith, in the distant days of his youth, had instructed him carefully in this matter. 'Mr Fred Smith,' he had been made to say, 'this is my Cousin Bertram who is a mortician.'
'Cousin Bertram who is a mortician this is Mr Fred Smith.'

And then they were supposed to shake hands. Or did that come first? Bootle awoke with a start. Someone — the Captain presumably — had asked him something. Well, there was only one safe answer; he never bothered to find another. It didn't make any difference anyway. 'Nothing to say, sir,' he mumbled, trying desperately to focus on his persecutors.

A moment later Bootle and his hook

were parted. A simple word from the Captain and he had lost the style and dignity of 'Leading Stoker Bootle' to become just plain 'Stoker Bootle'. (Bootle didn't hold with all this new-fangled nonsense about Stokers being called Mechanical Engineers or whatever. He had started life shovelling coal into the ancient boiler of a wartime minesweeper and was justly proud of his beginnings).

Except in the matter of pay, which in any case Bootle supplemented quietly in a number of ways, the disrating really made little difference. There was only one Bootle on board, for which mercy the Captain and Engineer Officer were profoundly grateful; and he retained the honorary and unofficial title of Chief Stoker's Mate which gave him power and influence far above any common old Leading hand. Besides he was older, smaller, oilier and gloomier than the rest. Bootle was *different*. The First Lieutenant, who was addicted to epigrams, once remarked that a crowd stood out from Bootle.

Still, losing a hook is a bother even if, with this possibility in mind, it is stitched on lightly with fine cotton. It made Bootle irritable and the black cloud which customarily accompanied him on his wanderings through the boat grew larger. With this and the stars which persisted in exploding in front of his red protesting eyes Bootle was in a bad way.

It seemed that not the smallest thing could go right. Searching for something to put out the fires which apparently raged inside him, he absent-mindedly switched on an empty tea-urn. Fortunately the Chief Electrician was taking it rather quietly after an evening ashore with the Chief Stoker; and the young electrician sent to repair the burnt-out boiler didn't presume to criticise the actions of an elderly Chief Stoker's Mate.

Meanwhile the Captain was shuffling through a batch of signals that had just arrived. A rather long one caught his eye. It was from the British Consul — a hard-pressed and normally pessimistic individual — at the port they had just left. It referred to Bootle's activities on the previous evening — the cause, ultimately, of his lost hook. It appeared that the account of the shore patrol who finally captured Bootle was substantially correct. There had indeed

been a beer-drinking contest (which Bootle had won) and there had indeed been a scuffle afterwards (which Bootle had not won). But it seemed that Bootle had taken part in the latter only to defend the honour of some French submariner acquaintances who were being called — on account of the Pom-Poms on their hats — undignified names by sailors from a certain aircraft carrier belonging to a certain mighty nation. Bootle thought his friends had not properly understood these insults in a strange language: but Bootle did and clearly it was his duty to take the matter up on his friends' behalf.

The Consul said that the newspapers had got hold of the story and that the battered Bootle was now the hero of the South of France. He ended his message with words to the effect that British prestige had never been higher and that hourly he expected word from the Elysèe Palace.

Preserving discipline

The Captain reflected soberly. Not for the first time Bootle had to get the right answer the wrong way. But he also suspected that the Hero of Southern France remembered little or nothing about the incident. As a matter of fact he was right. The Captain was a shrewd judge of human frailty. He decided that to acquaint Bootle now of his new-found popularity ashore might confuse a Leading Stoker's already limited understanding of naval justice. He would let it wait a day or so. Bootle's behaviour, however curious the consequences, had certainly merited the removal of his rate. Discipline had to be preserved.

The Captain's opinion was reinforced by an incident that morning in the Control Room. The ship's company had gone to action stations. Through the periscope could be seen a forest of masts of all shapes and sizes on the horizon. This was the blue NATO fleet which as a Red submarine (the colours chosen for each side in the exercise were, of course, quite arbitrary) the Captain had orders to attack.

It was at this moment that the main ballast pump decided to pack up. It had a habit of doing this and always chose its time with care. The Engineer Officer regarded it and its makers with deep personal loathing, but everyone knew the drill. Keeping the submarine at the

correct depth was now a great deal more difficult; the alternative pump was small and relatively slow. If the submarine grew heavy forward and light aft while the little pump was trying to do the work of its big brother and pump water out from a forward tank the First Lieutenant had to resort to old-fashioned — but effective — practices. The best way of coping with the situation was to broadcast the time-worn cry 'two fat seamen pass forward to aft — at the rush'. It was always diverting to see who responded loyally and promptly.

The engineers crowded round the ballast pump and soon had the offending portions of its bulky body lying in untidy heaps on the engine room deck. A gaping hole, leading down to the bilges, showed where they had come from. Then they set to work — but quietly because the noise of a hammer tapping, be it ever so gentle, can, of course, be heard for many miles under the sea. The Captain was not anxious to reveal the submarine's presence at this stage of the game. The first warning of a submarine — from a submariner's point of view — should be the arrival of a well-aimed torpedo. Absolute silence must be kept during the long stalk that precedes the kill.

Meanwhile it was Bootle's duty to raise and lower the periscope at the Captain's command — usually given by an economical gesture. It may not seem an onerous job but in fact the periscope operator is all important. Only the tip of the periscope must be allowed to appear above the surface — and then only for the least possible time. Today the periscope height had to be adjusted more frequently than usual; the difficulties in trimming without a ballast pump were causing the submarine to vary in depth by as much as six feet either side of the ideal periscope depth which the Captain had ordered.

All went well for a while. And then Bootle's attention — never fixed for long on anthing not connected with his personal well-being — wandered. The Captain gripped the periscope handles firmly and twisted them, trying to get a better view. He motioned with one finger. There was no response. Staring into the twin lenses he repeated the silent order. Still nothing happened.

'Up a bit'. This got through to Bootle instantly; he knew that tone. He had heard it before and it always meant trouble. He flung himself onto the periscope lever and pushed. Unfortunately he pushed it *down*.

A periscope, when it goes down, which it does quite briskly, vanishes neatly into a well just large enough to accommodate it. The well is not large enough to take a human body at the same time. If someone happens to be holding onto the handles when the periscope is lowered a conflict of priorities arises for the space available. The periscope, which weighs about one ton, is apt to win.

When the Captain had been hauled up and dusted down Bootle was relieved of his duties and invited to leave the Control Room. Nobody minded where he went (although some suggestions were made) as long as it was somewhere else. He took the hint.

Bootle reviewed the situation from the comparative safety of the galley where the chef — a kindly soul — could sometimes be persuaded to give temporary refuge to wanted men. Peering through the galley hatch he could see what was going on in the engine room. And he could see, too, a friendly looking hole in the deck plates which the offending ballast pump normally occupied. It would lead, as Bootle knew from experience of the nether regions, to a cosy little corner underneath the engines. He would never be found there; it was an ideal spot for a couple of hours' kip.

Bruised but recovered the Captain continued to direct the attack. He was encouraged to hear, as he manouevred his way stealthily towards the prime targets presented to him, that the ballast pump had been put together again. Then, as often happens during a submarine attack, the fleet — which was almost on top of him — turned away. He allowed himself a brief but pungent comment on luck, life and the tactics of the Blue Admiral.

Suddenly a violent noise broke out. Was somebody depth-charging the boat? The sonar operators had to remove their headphones to avoid being deafened. But it was not a depth-charge 'hammering' as wartime sub-mariners knew it. Bootle had woken up and found himself trapped. He was now calling attention to his situation with the aid of the large steel wheelspanner

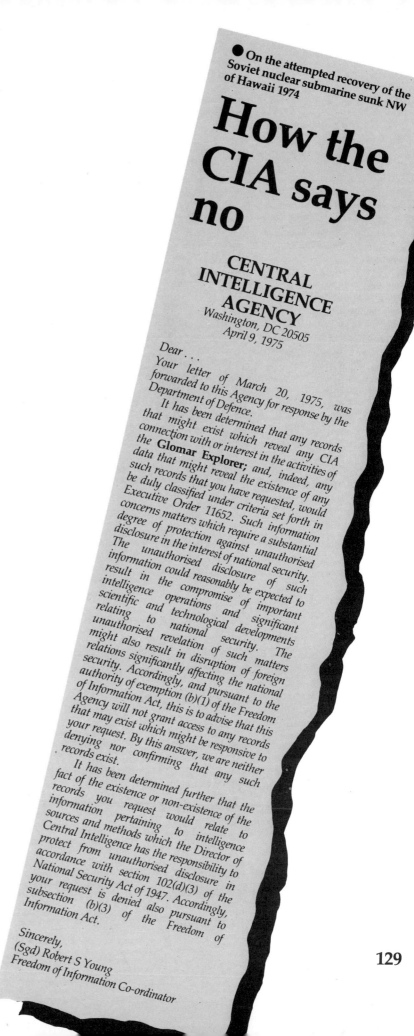

How the CIA says no

CENTRAL INTELLIGENCE AGENCY
Washington, DC 20505
April 9, 1975

Dear . . .

Your letter of March 20, 1975, was forwarded to this Agency for response by the Department of Defence.

It has been determined that any records that might exist which reveal any CIA connection with or interest in the activities of the **Glomar Explorer;** and, indeed, any data that might reveal the existence of any such records that you have requested, would be duly classified under criteria set forth in Executive Order 11652. Such information concerns matters which require a substantial degree of protection against unauthorised disclosure in the interest of national security. The unauthorised disclosure of such information could reasonably be expected to result in the compromise of important intelligence operations and significant scientific and technological developments relating to national security. The unauthorised revelation of such matters might also result in disruption of foreign relations significantly affecting the national security. Accordingly, and pursuant to the authority of exemption (b)(1) of the Freedom of Information Act, this is to advise that this Agency will not grant access to any records that may exist which might be responsive to your request. By this answer, we are neither denying nor confirming that any such records exist.

It has been determined further that the fact of the existence or non-existence of the records you request would relate to information pertaining to intelligence sources and methods which the Director of Central Intelligence has the responsibility to protect from unauthorised disclosure in accordance with section 102(d)(3) of the National Security Act of 1947. Accordingly, your request is denied also pursuant to subsection (b)(3) of the Freedom of Information Act.

Sincerely,
(Sgd) Robert S Young
Freedom of Information Co-ordinator

which he invariably carried as part of his accoutrements.

He was soon discovered and a dozen voices, appalled by the enormity of his crime, shouted at him to shut up. But they knew that the damage was done. The whole fleet must have heard the frantic knockings of a small, indignant, hungover Chief Stoker's Mate.

Odd things happen in submarines. By chance, Bootle's efforts saved the day. When a fleet steaming majestically along on a certain course hears unexpected underwater noises and doesn't know exactly where they come from it can only do one thing. It assumes that a submarine is at that moment in the dastardly act of firing torpedoes — and to spoil its aim everybody alters course. If they are clever all the ships do it together. In this case the whole fleet turned straight towards the Captain standing frustrated at the periscope.

When it was all over and two Blue aircraft carriers had been sent to the bottom (For Exercise, as the saying goes) the Captain sent for Bootle.

'Bootle,' he said sadly, 'you wouldn't understand but there are two reasons why, against my better judgement, I feel obliged to reward you.'

Dumbly Bootle accepted back the hook which he had only lost three hours before. He asked no questions. Officers were strange. You never knew what they would do next. Oddly enough, a little later in the wardroom, the Captain was saying much the same thing about Leading Stoker Bootle.

Some 60 Bootle stories have been broadcast on various radio networks at home and abroad.

The ups and downs of periscopes

THE FIRST INSPECTING captain of (British) submarines, Captain Reginald Bacon, claimed to have invented the periscope with the 15 feet ocular tube which he installed on *HM Submarine No 1 (Holland I)*; but in fact periscope devices were fitted to French submersibles for many years before *Holland I* slid down the slipway on October 2, 1901; while in America Simon Lake was developing his practical and effective omniscope which gave the user a nearly all-round view. However, Bacon's optical tube was undeniably the tallest instrument of the day and it enabled the British Holland boats to keep a satisfactory look-out while remaining submerged at a depth where the effects of sea and swell were considerably less marked than the virtually awash condition demanded by periscopes elsewhere. The first submarines in the US Navy lacked a periscope altogether and it was not until after the initial five *Adder*-class (following *USS Holland*) were commissioned that the first instrument was fitted to *USS Moccassin* using the port forward ventilator for the necessary hull penetration.

Incidentally, the American *Adder*-class Holland boats, before being fitted with periscopes, had to porpoise up and down to glimpse a target through the thick glass scuttles set into the short, heavy brass conning tower. Hence submarines in the USN for long were called pig-boats after the mariner's name for porpoises — sea pigs — and not because of living conditions on board!

Bacon's periscope lay, when not in use, flat along the casing and was raised and stayed like a mast when preparing to dive; there was no question of it being raised or lowered like a modern periscope. There was too little space in the early submarines to revolve the periscope eyepiece, particularly if the instrument was fitted in the conning tower itself, so the eyepiece remained fixed in the ahead position while the operator rotated the upper part of the

● The information about modern periscopes is supplied by Barr & Stroud, Caxton Street, Anniesland, Glasgow

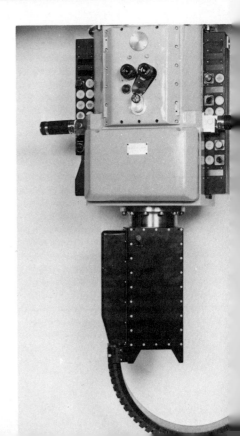

CK 34 search periscope with most mod cons

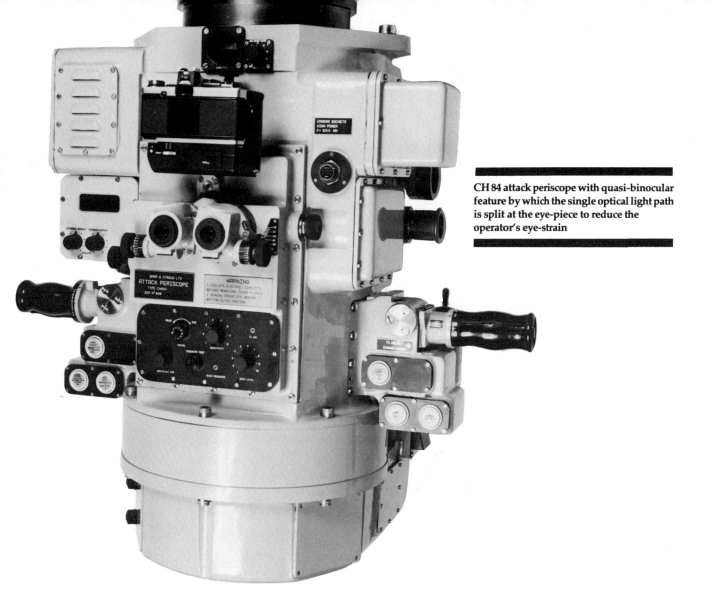

periscope tube by means of a handwheel. This had the effect of revolving the image so that it appeared upside down when astern and on end when abeam: although this would seem thoroughly undesirable today, commanding officers complained bitterly when the image was eventually righted — first by means of lenses (in *HMS A10*) and later by making the eyepiece and periscope rotatable together — because they could no longer judge the relative bearing at a glance!

So far as British periscopes are concerned Barr & Stroud took the lead about 70 years ago and their instruments in modern submarines would astonish submariners of older days. Their CK35 search and CH85 attack periscopes for the new RN 2400 class submarines and others are the latest in a long line of optics supplied to the Royal Navy. Incidentally, for some curious historical reason, the designation CH always refers to attack and CK to search periscopes.

Among the features of the CK35 and CH85 is a split eyepiece which gives a quasi-binocular effect to reduce the operator's eye-strain. Range from the estimator is calculated by a microprocessor and transmitted to the fire-control system. Target-height is set by another unit remote from the periscope. Target-designation letters and figures are injected into the eyepieces or on to off-mounted video monitors. Bearing transmission is derived from an optical encoder in the crosshead and true bearing is displayed in the left eyepiece as well as remotely.

A laser rangefinder can be fitted in attack periscopes, and utilises proven Nd: YAG modules. Accurate collimation is maintained with the aiming mark in the optical image intensification of thermal imaging systems. The line of sight is stabilised to assist the operation. Accuracy is ± 10m. Range to target is displayed in the eyepiece and can be transmitted to the fire-control system.

The AHPS4 artificial horizon sextant includes a stabilised mirror coupled to the submarine's compass or inertial navigation system (SINS) and controls are kept simple to allow a sight to be taken within a few seconds. There is provision for automatic removal of errors in the observed altitude caused by bending of the periscope or distortion of the boat's structure. A printout provides the observed altitude, bearing and time of observation. The top window and eyepiece are heated, and this is controlled by a solid-state unit in the periscope. A motor in the crosshead rotates the periscope without manual assistance by the operator or it can be rotated remotely from a Tactical TV Console (TTVC)

Modern search periscopes can be fitted with Electronic Support Measures (ESM) and it is known that Racal-Decca has a contract to supply submarine ESM equipment to the Navy. It provides omni-directional warning, directional indication and analysis of incoming signals with threat-assessment. An active receive radio antenna is also fitted with whatever frequency coverage is required.

Both periscopes can be fitted with an Olympus OM2 35mm still camera, with up to 250 frames and control is by means of a button near the right-hand training handle. A Polaroid camera can also be fitted.

The Navy has not yet stated a preference for the alternatives of an image-intensifier or a thermal imager, but either option is available on these periscopes.

The Barr & Stroud image-intensifier uses a Mullard 50/40 Type XX 1332 tube which gives a luminous gain of up to 30,000x, equivalent to near-starlight, with high resolution. It requires an additional 110mm diameter window in the top of the main tube. The thermal imager uses a 110mm germanium window at the top of the main tube, and the thermal picture can be viewed in the eyepiece or relayed to a remote monitor and/or video tape recorder. The thermal imager used is the Barr & Stroud IR18 MK 2, giving a CCIR compatible video output, and the module is located at the top of the main periscope tube, operating in the 8-13 micron waveband.

The thermal imager gives the periscope day and night capability and enhances its detection and identification in haze, mist or sun glare. The operator views the thermal scene at the eyepiece, using controls to adjust sensitivity, grey level and focus. The video signal is taken to the remote monitor and video recorder, where a polarity invert switch is also provided.

A 16mm SIT Videcon TV camera, fitted at the rear of the ocular box, relays the optical, image-intensifier or thermal imager picture to a remote monitor and/or video tape recorder, with provision for alphanumeric insertion of data.

Both periscopes are fitted with standard anti-vibration optics, to minimise the effect of vibration on the stability of the picture, and they have facilities for desiccation using the submarine's high pressure air system.

These instruments are designed to operate satisfactorily at submerged speeds up to 16 knots. Most periscope functions can be controlled by an operator seated at the TTVC located adjacent to other sensor displays in the control room; when in the remote control mode there is no necessity to have an operator at the periscope.

Today's periscopes are much more than a mere optical aid to the commanding officer: they are sensors in their own right and are far removed from Captain Bacon's optical tube.

The stayed-mast type of early periscope fitted to the Holland boats built in 1901-02. Incidentally, all the crew of No 4 are on deck here except for one (and, of course, the three white mice hung up in a cage below by the engine to give warning of carbon monoxide poisoning)

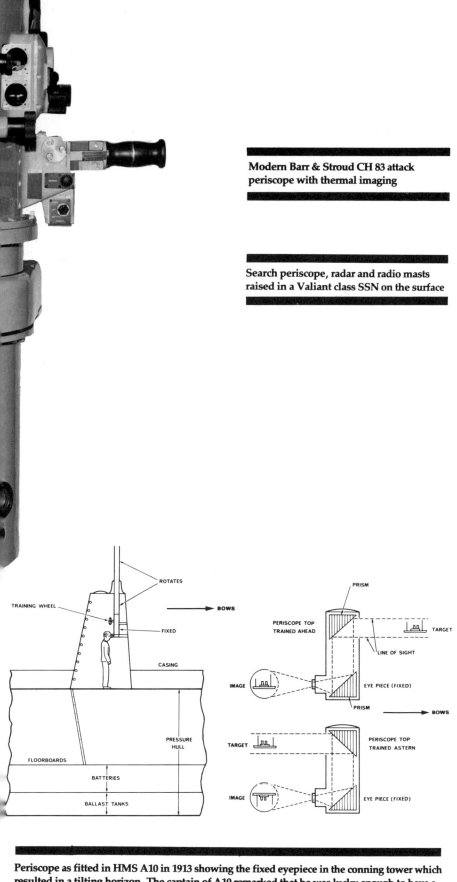

Modern Barr & Stroud CH 83 attack periscope with thermal imaging

Search periscope, radar and radio masts raised in a Valiant class SSN on the surface

ROTATES

TRAINING WHEEL

FIXED

BOWS

CASING

PRESSURE HULL

FLOORBOARDS

BATTERIES

BALLAST TANKS

PRISM

PERISCOPE TOP
TRAINED AHEAD

LINE OF SIGHT

TARGET

IMAGE

EYE PIECE (FIXED)

PRISM

BOWS

TARGET

PERISCOPE TOP
TRAINED ASTERN

IMAGE

EYE PIECE (FIXED)

Periscope as fitted in HMS A10 in 1913 showing the fixed eyepiece in the conning tower which resulted in a tilting horizon. The captain of A10 remarked that he was lucky enough to have a very small stoker who perched above him in the tower and operated the upper-tube training wheel, calling out the bearing as required. In the right hand diagram an attempt is made to show why the image of the target becomes inverted when the periscope top is trained astern

Typical attack periscope fitted in RN submarines between the first and second world wars, shown here in an H boat. The hoist wires frayed quite rapidly and the job of replacing them at sea was dirty, difficult and a considerable operational hindrance

A view from the surface

● By Rear Admiral Richard Hill

AT THE END of a chilly, westerly day off Portland, a day of basic anti-submarine operator training, my frigate had gone through the standard surfacing procedures; the submarine had surfaced, and we set off through the murk, northbound for Portland harbour between the West Shambles Buoy and the Bill.

'No need to send a signal to the submarines,' said my Captain, 'they follow you like dogs'. We huddled deeper into our duffle coats on the open bridge until visibility lifted a bit. 'My God', said the Captain, peering aft, 'there's a pack of three of them now . . .'

That was in 1953 when submarine navigation was regarded by surface ships as a joke. Submariners, of course, would seldom admit to surface ship people that they were uncertain of their position for they tried very hard to be in the right place at the right time. But anyone who had tried to swing a submarine's magnetic compass ('Faithful Fred') for deviation, or correct side error in its periscope sextant, knew their difficulties.

In large-scale exercises navigational errors could lead to a reduction in useful encounters and to terrible problems in analysis afterwards. The fault wasn't always the submariner's. I recall an exercise in the Mediterranean where the Officer in Tactical Command (not British, I'm glad to say) steered 270° to make good 270° in a full southerly gale. We made 17 miles leeway in as many hours and missed the waiting submarines which were in their allocated patrol areas. As for aircraft navigational errors, they were notorious. The average datum error in one exercise in the mid-50s I worked out as ten miles.

Exercise analysis in these circumstances was an art as much as a science. The navigational data, too, were only part of the problem. Disagreements

Anti-submarine warfare (ASW) is a percentage game, requiring a variety of systems and defence in depth. A Sea King helicopter prepared to dip its sonar. HMS Hermes (before modernisation) in the background

across the air-sea interface went on well after the pinging had stopped. Oh no, said one submariner at a 'wash-up', I was ten miles to the south; they must have been hunting a non-sub contact, those destroyers. Well, said the destroyer men, waving their range recorder traces, what's all this then? The polite arguments went on (Flag Officer Flotillas was present) and were unresolved. At the coffee break I asked the navigator of the submarine 'Why *did* you go deep at 1016?' He smiled and broke off the conversation.

So the surface view of submariners, uncharitably expressed, was that they didn't know; you couldn't tell them; and they were a devious lot anyway. Charitably put, of course, it was quite different: with all their limitations, they were vastly professional lone predators, to be feared and respected by surface ships.

It has all changed now, I suppose. Nuclear-powered for the most part, the submarine forces of the major navies are equipped for battle in dimensions to which their predecessors could not aspire except by chance: submerged submarine versus submarine, missile-armed submarine versus surface ship at long range, submerged submarine co-operating with surface units and aircraft. The Ships Inertial Navigation System (SINS) and navigational satellites have taken much of the inaccuracy out of ocean navigation, and pilotage waters matter less to the nuclear submarine than the conventional. Improved hydrophone arrays, Fast Fourier Transform techniques and self-noise reduction have helped to improve and clarify the sonic information available. Advances in oceanography have given submarines the tools whereby they can best position themselves to avoid detection. Communications across the sea-air interface are better than they were. Torpedoes and missiles are intelligent and highly lethal, demanding tactical skills of the order needed only to fire them into high-probability areas.

So there is much ground on which to

Submarines are simply inappropriate for certain types of operation, such as the Gulf of Oman patrol

base the claim that the nuclear-powered submarine is today's capital ship, an expression as difficult to define as Sea Power or Command of the Sea, but however one analyses it in terms of submarines it is a thought too glib. The fleet submarine is an offensive weapon system of great power and survivability, an ideal unit for exercising sea denial, but if it attempts to control the surface it is acting out of character and temporarily loses its advantages. As so much of western defence philosophy is founded on the need to get cargoes across the sea, and since there is no prospect of cargoes going beneath the surface, that limitation is vital.

So also is the inappropriateness of submarines, and nuclear-powered submarines in particular, for not-quite-peace operations that obstinately refuse to disappear despite the pundits' reiteration that 'the days of gunboat diplomacy are over'. The Gulf of Oman Patrol is a modern instance, but in truth navies have been occupied in them in one part of the world or another for a long time. Regulation of coastal waters is another thing that submarines cannot do efficiently. Finally, the Falklands Campaign showed dramatically that in certain circumstances the brunt of the action simply has to be borne by surface forces because submarines can neither carry a lot of troops and supplies, nor counter air threats.

It is more rational, therefore, to regard submarines as a powerful arm of a balanced maritime force — an arm which, even if it is not in active use, will always be known by an opponent to exist, and which therefore will be a powerful deterrent. Of course, if a nation should decide not to have a balanced maritime force — if, for example, it foolishly bases its defence provision on a single scenario — then it might put more emphasis on submarines. Even in these circumstances however, it would have to be certain of its tactical doctrine, and the way in which future developments

The often-heard claim that 'the nuclear-powered submarine is today's capital ship' is, on any analysis, a trifle too glib: the Soviet Charlie class pictured here is a formidable, but not a dominant, weapon system

would affect that doctrine, before staking all on its submarine force.

Here the surface practitioner finds himself returning to ancient scepticisms. A few paragraphs back I listed all the improvements to the tactical abilities of submarines in the past 20 years — except that I did not mention the most important, the independence of the surface that nuclear power confers. It is a vastly impressive list. Yet one must wonder whether the improvements are so comprehensive as claimed.

To take underwater sensors first, the improvements in passive listening and analysis techniques are often reported as though a submarine was now aware, from deep, of everything going on in the depths and on the surface for a distance of tens of miles round it. To me this sounds suspiciously like the reliance placed on Asdic before World War II, when — basing their opinion on the results of unrealistic exercises in good water conditions — the naval staff assumed that any submarine within detection range would be detected, attacked and sunk. There is a fascinating file in the Public Records Office dated 1936 about a 'B' class destroyer on the Nyon Patrol which attacked a contact, and failed to kill. Agonising went on for months: if it wasn't a submarine why was it classified as such? If it was a submarine why wasn't it destroyed? Lord Chatfield closed the file with a memorable one-liner, 'It was not a submarine. — C.' Experience in World War II makes such agonising look absurd: anti-submarine warfare, like submarine warfare, was seen to be a percentage game, as it still is. But it is difficult to cull the right percentages from artificial exercises: claims to infallibility or thereabouts must be taken with a pinch of salt. It is not a measure, although an indication, of the fallibility of sonic information that at least two submarines have been caught in fishing nets in the past two years.

History can probably teach us something, too, when it comes to weaponry. Take torpedoes whose record as a ready weapon at the beginning of conflict, is appalling. Failure rates of 50% were reported by German and American submarines at the start of World War II. This is, mind you, a figure for *technical* failure: not keeping the set depth, deviating off

course and, worst, not detonating when they hit. No doubt modern torpedoes are more extensively tested than were the German ones in the 30s: but there is a lot more to go wrong. I had a small bet with myself when the *General Belgrano* was sunk that it would have been with the 50-year-old, well-tried Mark 8** rather than the clever Mark 24 as the press instantly speculated. Judging by later reports, I won that bet.

Missiles may demonstrate more reliability. Certainly their trials (much more fully reported than torpedo trials) suggest that conclusion, as does the performances of Exocet and Sea Skua in the Falklands. These were of course air-launched missiles, but the arrangements for submerged launch of missiles such as Harpoon seem to have given little trouble. The fact that such missiles are generally fired from a reasonably tranquil tactical environment, with the submarine probably not under immediate threat, may improve the certainty of the preparation and firing sequence. However a long firing range presents another kind of problem to the submarine, for it is outside any precise target location that could be achieved under normal circumstances by the submarine's own sensors. Either the submarine must be told, through the sea-air interface or by some ship or aircraft above it, just where the target is; or it must fire, on directional information only, 'into the brown'; or it must wait for

The Ikara long range ASW missile is launched from a surface vessel to deliver a homing torpedo. The torpedo dropping position is computed from sonar and other sources and a guidance system controls flight to the dropping point where the torpedo is released on a parachute. The system is in service with the Royal and Royal Australian navies and a variant is now installed in four Brazilian frigates

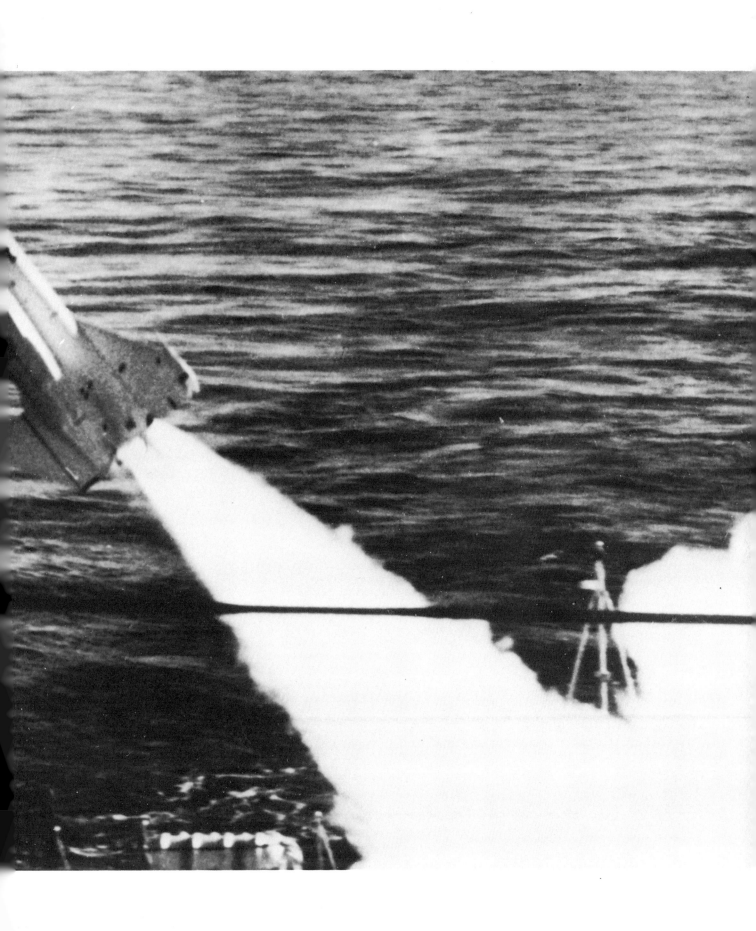

more precise information as the range closes.

Communications across the sea-air interface historically have been difficult for only very low radio frequencies reach a deep submarine. Communications on the higher frequencies, which alone can carry enough data for tactical co-operation with surface ships or aircraft, demand an aerial close to the surface if not actually breaking it. This clearly means exposure of the submarine, though it may not be serious; it depends on the threat, and also on what the submarine is trying to do. The alternative of sonic communication by underwater telephone used to be one of the jollier interludes of a surface ship operations officer's life. Those strange, burbling words that went out into the watery abyss, usually with no response from the submarine, gave an other-wordly feel to the whole exercise which was amusing so long as the reason for the call was unimportant.

The sense of achievement when things go right may make one forget how often they go wrong, and wartime conditions make them go wrong more often. This is a percentage game too; those pinning their faith in, for example, Nimrod — SSN co-operation in the Greenland-Iceland-UK gaps should take a cool look at the proportion of occasions on which communication is achieved — and then halve it to get a wartime figure.

I suppose the sceptical surface mariner's message from the preceding paragraphs is simply that no system is infallible, and submarines are no exception. But even less would those on the surface (and, I hope, in the air) claim high efficiencies for their own anti-submarine measures. The wisest thing I ever heard said about ASW was by a great scientist who had not previously been exposed to maritime matters but had heard with great patience some partisan presentations from naval and air staffs. 'Well,' he said, 'it seems to me that the only answer is to have all systems operating. Then you may have a chance'.

The components of the anti-submarine forces are well enough known. Fixed-wing aircraft mainly have sonobuoy sensors, sophisticated onboard data processing, and torpedoes and depth charges. In addition

helicopters can put an active sonar in the water, but their endurance is less. Surface ships can tow passive arrays (a recent development whose potential is immense but largely untried) but their active sonar is of relatively short reach. Submarines are said by some to be the best anti-submarine vehicles of all, but to be at their best they need quiet water.

It is not so much that each component fits conveniently into a slot geographically and tactically marked out for it, as that each can be expected to contribute to the attrition of an opposing submarine force. So it was in 1943, when a whole set of parallel developments in anti-submarine equipment and oper-ational doctrine turned the situation round between the end of February and the end of May. But that was three and a half years into a long hard war, with the benefit of experience and unremitting work by scientists and researchers. An anti-submarine battle in the future might give us three and a half days, three and a half weeks if we were lucky, to learn our lessons before the crucial phase. Doubtless there would be some unpleasant surprises: would, for example, predeployment of opposing submarines pre-empt any attempt to dispute the passage of the gaps? How fiercely would long-range maritime patrol aircraft be attacked? How early would the opposition use nuclear weapons?

It seems to me that, given such vast areas of doubt, the West should give up no element of its anti-submarine effort, nor attenuate it too much in favour of other elements. All computations of the relative efficiencies of the components will depend on data of doubtful accuracy under realistic conditions, and may well be over-dependent on a scenario which turns out to be wrong or assumptions not borne out in practise. (I recall one sea-battle fought at the Defence Operational Analysis Estab-lishment in which it was assumed that if the positions of the forces indicated an encounter, such encounter would take

RN ratings have just clipped the wings and tail fins on to the Ikara rocket body

place: which led to the dictum that 'The sky is always blue over West Byfleet'.)

What one can plan for, though, is to impose on enemy submarines the maximum need to expose themselves if they are to get into a firing position. To use speed, to come above the layer, to communicate, to transmit on active sonar: these are things no submariner wants if he can get in an attack without. But a judicious mixture of convoys, independently routed fast merchant ships, and support groups, all steering courses to make the most confusing sonic picture possible — firmly organised by the excellent command, control and information systems available to the West both ashore and afloat — could force many opposing submarines to do what they don't want to.

Nor should it be forgotten that once it has attacked, a submarine is in an exposed position. No doubt it is satisfying to a submariner to fire a green grenade (if that is what they still do to indicate a simulated torpedo attack) undetected, and in war it would be even more so. But the number of unalerted detections by escorts and support groups in World War II was not, I suspect, all that large; yet more than 700 U-boats were sunk. Surface ships therefore should not get too much of an inferiority complex; a burning datum is not a pretty sight, but it has led to many a successful anti-submarine hunt.

If there is a message from these ramblings from the other side of the interface, it is Balance. No, I do not think that submarine-versus-submarine is the biggest con-job since Cagliostro (though it was a now very senior submariner who told me that, after the fourth glass of Ministry of Defence rotgut sherry); nor do I think that Nimrod has been spoon-fed on simple targets and will anyway run out of sonobuoys on day two (though there are worrying truths behind both statements); nor do I expect surface ships in difficult conditions to obtain sonar detections at maximum range. I do thing that going overboard for a single panacea, particularly on a single scenario, is disastrous silliness; so let us continue searching for defence in depth. Oh, and I also still think that our submariners are a devious lot. But as long as they are on our side, that's all right.

Victoria Crosses for submariners

1 December 22, 1914, Lieutenant N D Holbrook, RN *'for most conspicuous bravery on December 13, when in command of the Submarine BII, he entered the Dardanelles, and, notwithstanding the very difficult current, dived his vessel under five rows of mines and torpedoed the Turkish battleship Messudiyeh, which was guarding the mine-field.*

'Lieutenant Holbrook succeeded in bringing the BII safely back, although assailed by gun-fire and torpedo boats, having been submerged on one occasion for nine hours.'

2 May 21, 1915, Commander E C Boyle, RN *'for most conspicuous bravery, in command of Submarine E14, when he dived his vessel under the enemy minefields and entered the Sea of Marmara on April 17, 1915. In spite of great navigational difficulties from strong currents, of the continual neighbourhood of hostile patrols, and of the hourly danger of attack from the enemy, he continued to operate in the narrow waters of the Straits and succeeded in sinking two Turkish gunboats and one large military transport.'*

3 June 24, 1915, Lieutenant Commander M E Naismith, RN *'for most conspicuous bravery in command of one of His Majesty's Submarines while operating in the Sea of Marmora. In the face of great danger he succeeded in destroying one large Turkish gunboat, two transports, one ammunition ship and three store-ships, in addition to driving one store-ship ashore. When he had safely passed the most difficult part of his homeward journey he returned again to torpedo a Turkish transport.'*

4 July 23, 1918, Lieutenant R D Sandford, RN. *'This officer was in command of Submarine C3, and most skilfully placed that vessel in between the piles of the viaduct before lighting his fuse and abandoning her. He eagerly undertook this hazardous enterprise, although well aware (as were all his crew) that if the means of rescue failed and he or any of his crew were in the water at the moment of the explosion, they could be killed outright by the force of such explosion. Yet Lieutenant Sandford disdained to use the gyro steering, which would have enabled him and his crew to abandon the submarine at a safe distance, and preferred to make sure, as far as was humanly possible, of the accomplishment of his duty.'* At Zeebrugge.

● Altogether 14 VCs have been awarded to submariners. Chronologically their recipients were:

5 May 24, 1919, Lieutenant Commander G S White, RN. *'E14 left Mudros on January 27 under instructions to force the narrows and attack the Goeben, which was reported aground off Nagara Point after being damaged during her sortie from the Dardanelles. The later vessel was not found and E14 turned back. At about 8.45 am on January 28 a torpedo was fired from E14 at an enemy ship; II seconds after the torpedo left the tube a heavy explosion took place, caused all lights to go out, and sprang the fore hatch. Leaking badly the boat was blown to 15 feet, and at once a heavy fire came from the forts, but the hull was not hit. E14 then dived and proceeded on her way out.*

'Soon afterwards the boat became out of control and as the air supply was nearly exhausted, Lieutenant Commander White decided to run the risk of proceeding on the surface. Heavy fire was immediately opened from both sides, and, after running the gauntlet for half-an-hour, being steered from below, E14 was so badly damaged that Lieutenant Commander White turned towards the shore in order to give the crew a chance of being saved. He remained on deck the whole time himself until he was killed by a shell.'

6 December 16, 1941, Lieutenant Commander M D Wanklyn, DSO, RN. *'On the evening of May 24, 1941, while on patrol off the coast of Sicily, Lieutenant Commander Wanklyn, in command of His Majesty's Submarine Upholder, sighted a south-bound enemy troop-convoy, strongly escorted by Destroyers. The failing light was such that observation by periscope could not be relied on but a surface attack would have been easily seen. Upholder's listening gear was out of action.*

'In spite of these severe handicaps Lieutenant Commander Wanklyn decided to press home his attack at short range. He quickly steered his craft into a favourable position and closed in so as to make sure of his target. By this time the whereabouts of the escorting Destroyers could not be made out. Lieutenant Commander Wanklyn, while fully aware of the risk of being rammed by one of the escorts, continued to press on towards the enemy troop-ships. As he was about to fire, one of the enemy destroyers suddenly appeared out of the darkness at high speed, and he only just avoided being rammed. As soon as he was clear, he brought his periscope sights on and fired torpedoes, which sank a large troop-ship. The enemy Destroyers at once made a strong counter-attack and during the next 20 minutes dropped 37 depth-charges near Upholder.

'The failure of his listening devices made it much harder for him to get away, but with the greatest courage, coolness and skill he brought Upholder clear of the enemy and safe back to harbour. Before this outstanding attack, and since being appointed a Companion of the Distinguished Service Order, Lieutenant Commander Wanklyn has torpedoed a tanker and a merchant vessel.

'He has continued to show the utmost bravery in the presence of the enemy. He has carried out his attacks on enemy vessels with skill and relentless determination, and has also sunk one Destroyer, one U-boat, two troop-transports of 19,500 tons each, one tanker and three supply ships. He has besides probably destroyed by torpedoes one Cruiser and one Destroyer, and possibly hit another Cruiser.'

7 & 8 June 9, 1942, Lieutenant P S W Roberts, RN and Petty Officer T W Gould. *'On February 16, in daylight, H M Submarine Thrasher attacked and sank a heavily escorted supply ship. She was at once attacked by depth-charges and was bombed by aircraft. The presence of two unexploded bombs in the gun-casing was discovered when after dark the submarine surfaced and began to roll.*

'Lieutenant Roberts and Petty Officer Gould volunteered to remove the bombs, which were of a type unknown to them. The danger in dealing with the second bomb was very great. To reach it they had to go through the casing which was so low that they had to lie at full length to move in it. Through this narrow space, in complete darkness, they pushed and dragged the bomb for a distance of some 20 feet until it could be lowered over the side. Every time the bomb was moved there was a loud twanging noise as of a broken spring which added nothing to their peace of mind.

'This deed was the more gallant as H M Submarine Thrasher's presence was known to the enemy; she was close to the enemy coast, and in waters where his patrols were known to be active day and night. There was

a very great chance, and they knew it, that the submarine might have to crash-dive while they were in the casing. Had this happened they must have been drowned.'

9 July 7, 1942, Commander A C C Miers, DSO., RN *'for valour in command of H M Submarine Torbay in a daring and successful raid on shipping in a defended enemy harbour, planned with full knowledge of the great hazards to be expected during 17 hours in waters closely patrolled by the enemy. On arriving in the harbour he had to charge his batteries lying on the surface in full moonlight, under the guns of the enemy. As he could not see his target he waited several hours and attacked in full daylight in a glassy calm. When he had fired his torpedoes he was heavily counter-attacked and had to withdraw through a long channel with anti-submarine craft all round and continuous air patrols overhead.'*

10 May 25, 1943, Commander J W Linton, DSO., RN. *'From the outbreak of War until HMS Turbulent's last patrol Commander Linton was constantly in command of submarines, and during that time inflicted great damage on the enemy. He sank one Cruiser, one Destroyer, one U-boat, 28 Supply Ships, some 100,000 tons in all,*

and destroyed three trains by gunfire. In his last year he spent 254 days at sea, submerged for nearly half the time, and his ship was hunted 13 times and had 250 depth-charges aimed at her.

'His many and brilliant successes were due to his constant activity and skill, and the daring which never failed him when there was an enemy to be attacked. On one occasion, for instance, in HMS Turbulent, he sighted a convoy of two Merchantment and two Destroyers in mist and moonlight. He worked round ahead of the convoy and dived to attack it as it passed through the moon's rays. On bringing his sights to bear he found himself right ahead of a Destroyer. Yet he held his course till the Destroyer was almost on top of him, and, when his sights came on the convoy, he fired. His great courage and determination were rewarded. He sank one Merchantman and one Destroyer outright, and set the other Merchantman on fire so that she blew up.'

11, 12 February 22, 1944, Lieutenant B C G Place, DSC., RN and Lieutenant D Cameron, RNR. *'Lieutenants Place and Cameron were the Commanding Officers of two of His Majesty's Midget Submarines X7 and X6 which on September 22, 1943 carried out a most daring and successful attack on the German Battleship Tirpitz, moored in the*

protected anchorage of Kaa fjord, North Norway. To reach the anchorage necessitated the penetration of an enemy mine-field and a passage of 50 miles up the fjord, known to be vigilantly patrolled by the enemy and to be guarded by nets, gun defences and listening posts, this after a passage of at least a thousand miles from base.

'Having successfully eluded all these hazards and entered the fleet anchorage, Lieutenants Place and Cameron, with a complete disregard for danger, worked their small craft past the close anti-submarine and torpedo nets surrounding the Tirpitz, and from a position inside these nets, carried out a cool and determined attack. Whilst they were still inside the nets a fierce enemy counter attack by guns and depth-charges developed which made their withdrawal impossible. Lieutenants Place and Cameron therefore scuttled their craft to prevent them falling into the hands of the enemy. Before doing so they took every measure to ensure the safety of their crews, the majority of whom, together with themselves, were subsequently taken prisoner.

'In the course of the operation these small craft pressed home their attack to the full, in doing so accepting all the dangers inherent in such vessels and facing every possible hazard which ingenuity could devise for the protection in harbour of vitally important Capital Ships. The courage, endurance and

One of the first aircraft-carriers was a submarine. HMS E22, completed in 1915 (and torpedoed by U18 in 1916), carried two Sopwith Schneiders. The boat trimmed down to float off the seaplanes and, if weather conditions were ideal, recovered them similarly. The object was to make bombing raids on German Zeppelin bases at Tondern and Cuxhaven but there is no record of a successful operation. Unable to dive with the machines embarked, E22 was particularly vulnerable. A Hythe camera gun is fitted on the rear aircraft in this rare photograph

utter contempt for danger in the immediate face of the enemy shown by Lieutenants Place and Cameron during this determined and successful attack were supreme.'

13 November 13, 1945, Lieutenant I E Fraser, DSC., RNR. *'Lieutenant Fraser commanded H M Midget Submarine XE3 in a successful attack on a Japanese heavy cruiser of the Atago class at her moorings in Johore Strait, Singapore, on July 31, 1945. During the long approach up the Singapore Straits XE3 deliberately left the believed safe channel and entered mined waters to avoid suspected hydrophone posts. The target was aground, or nearly aground, both fore and aft, and only under the midship portion was there just sufficient water for XE3 to place herself under the cruiser. For 40 minutes XE3 pushed her way along the sea-bed until finally Lieutenant Fraser managed to force her right under the centre of the cruiser. Here he placed the limpets and dropped his main side charge. Great difficulty was experienced in extricating the craft after the attack had been completed, but finally XE3 was clear, and commenced her long return journey out*

to sea. The courage and determination of Lieutenant Fraser are beyond all praise. Any man not possessed of his relentless determination to achieve his object in full, regardless of all consequences, would have dropped his side charge alongside the target instead of persisting until he had forced his submarine right under the cruiser. The approach and withdrawal entailed a passage of 80 miles through water which had been mined by both the enemy and ouselves, past hydrophone positions, over loops and controlled mine-fields, and through an anti-submarine boom.'

14 Temporary Acting Leading Seaman J J Magennis. *'Leading Seaman Magennis served as Diver in H M Midget Submarine XE3 for her attack on July 31, 1945, on a Japanese cruiser of the Atago class. Owing to the fact that XE3 was tightly jammed under the target the diver's hatch could not be fully opened, and Magennis had to squeeze himself through the narrow space available.*

'He experienced great difficulty in placing his limpets on the bottom of the cruiser owing both to the foul state of the bottom and to the

pronounced slope upon which the limpets would not hold. Before a limpet could be placed therefore Magennis had thoroughly to scrape the area clear of barnacles and in order to secure the limpets he had to tie them in pairs by a line passing under the cruiser's keel. This was very tiring work for a diver and he was moreover handicapped by a steady leakage of oxygen which was ascending in bubbles to the surface. A lesser man would have been content to place a few limpets and then return to the craft. Magennis, however, persisted until he had placed his full outfit before returning to the craft in an exhausted condition. Shortly after withdrawing Lieutenant Fraser endeavoured to jettison his limpet carriers, but one of these would not release itself and fall clear of the craft. Despite his exhaustion, his oxygen leak and the fact that there was every probability of his being sighted, Magennis at once volunteered to leave the craft and free the carrier rather than allow a less experienced diver to undertake the job. After seven minutes of nerve-racking work he succeeded in releasing the carrier. Magennis displayed very great courage and devotion to duty and complete disregard for his own safety.'

Further reading

Alden, J D *The Fleet Submarine in the USN* — US Naval Institute Press, 1979

Bagnasco, E *Submarines of World War Two* — Arms and Armour Press, 1977

Blair, C *Silent Victory, The US submarine war against Japan* — J B Lippincott, 1975

Compton-Hall, R *Submarine Boats* — The beginnings of underwater warfare, Conway Maritime 1983, £10.50

Compton-Hall, R *Submarines* — for schools and young people, Wayland, 1982 £4.25

Compton-Hall, R *The Underwater War 1939-1945* — Blandford, 1982 £8.95

Gallagher, T *Against All Odds* — Midget submarines against the *Tirpitz*, Macdonald, 1971 £1.75

Horton, E *The Illustrated History of the Submarine* — Sidgwick and Jackson, 1974 £3.50

● Regrettably there have been a few books published on submarines in recent years which are written with insufficient knowledge of the subject: some are misleading and inaccurate. However the following books are amongst those which are reliable and recommended. The list is not, of course, exhaustive and the fact that any book is not included certainly does not imply that it falls into the 'unreliable' category: the reader must be the judge of that. Prices are given, where known, at the time of publication

Herzog, B *60 Jahre Deutsche U-Boote 1906-1966* — (in German) J F Lehmanns Verlag, 1968

le Masson, H *Du Nautilus (1800) au Redoubtable* — (in French) Presses de la Cité, 1969

Lipscomb, Cdr F W *The British Submarine* — Conway Maritime 1975, £6.50

Morris, R K *John P Holland* — US Naval Institute Press, 1965

Preston, A (ill J Batchelor) *Submarines The History and Evolution of Underwater Fighting Vessels,* — Phoebus/BPC 1975 £2.50

Rössler, E *Die Deutschen U-Boote und ihre Werften* — (in German) 2 volumes, Bernard and Graefe Verlag, 1979

Rössler, E *The U-Boat* The Evolution and technical history of German Submarines — Arms & Armour Press, 1981 £27.50

Showell, J P M *U-Boats under the Swastika* — Ian Allan, 1973, £4.50